birdwatching

with your

eyes closed

an introduction to birdsong

SIMON BARNES

with illustrations by Alex Fox

Published in 2011 by Short Books
3a Exmouth House
Pine Street
EC1R 0JH
2 3 4 5 6 7 8 9 10

A CIP catalogue record for this book
is available from the British Library.

ISBN 978-1-907595-47-9

Printed and bound by
CPI Group (UK) Ltd, Croydon, CR0 4YY

For Jeremy Sorensen and Bob Stjernstedt who lent me their ears

and for CLW who sometimes listens with me

Contents

Contents

birdwatching

with your
eyes closed:

podcast, and other resources

You can hear the birds speaking for themselves on a podcast designed to accompany this book. It includes sounds from all 66 species described in these pages plus a brief spoken introduction to each species from me, with pointers that will, I hope, help with identification. You can find this at www.shortbooks.co.uk – if you don't know what a podcast is, a helpful young person will burn it onto a CD for you.

If you google the name of a British bird, you will be directed to the RSPB website's account of that species, which includes a brief clip of birdsound; a very helpful resource. There are also comprehensive descriptions plus CDs of all British birds in the excellent *Collins Bird Songs & Calls* by Geoff Sample. A considerable range of recordings of birdsound and other natural noises can be bought from www.wildsounds.co.uk, who worked on the podcast that comes with this book.

First Winter

Muzak to my ears

Imagine you are sitting in a pub. I expect most people's imagination can stretch that far, but if you have a problem, imagine you're in a coffee-shop or something. The important thing is that they are piping in music over the loudspeakers.

But you haven't noticed that. It's not that you haven't noticed which song they're playing; you haven't noticed that they're playing music at all. It's just a background blur. You read your paper, you wait for your friend, or you talk to your companion, unaware that you've raised your voice in order to be heard above the music.

Then suddenly you realise they are playing That Song. You know the one. The one you heard when you first met. Suddenly the melody cuts through the fug and reaches your conscious mind. Yes, that time, when it was all so crazy and so wonderful, that precarious time of fearful joy.

Suddenly the sound, and with it the place and the time, is charged with meaning. Suddenly, out of the background blur, a vital message is imparted. Suddenly every sense is awake. Every note, every instrument, every word *matters*. It's like a personal message, even though you know it came from whatever impersonal system it is that chooses music in pubs. Suddenly the place is alive. Suddenly, you are alive.

I want you to have this experience, not for the duration of the song and its afterglow, but for the rest of your life. Every time you walk into a wood or along the seashore, every time you take a detour through the park on the way to work, every time you sit in the garden, the sounds around you will become charged with meaning. And every bird is singing your song.

Songs of life and death

Birds sing. Each species sings a different song. That's quite interesting for the human being who happens to be listening, but it's life and death for the bird. When a bird sings, it sings the song of itself. The first and most basic piece of information that the song conveys is which species the bird belongs to. There is no point in a blackbird singing a lovesong to a wren: a young man might just as well present a bunch of flowers to an orang-utan. It is important *for a blackbird* that a blackbird sounds like a blackbird.

A willow warbler looks almost exactly the same as a chiffchaff. As a general rule, a chiffchaff will have darker legs, but that's hard to see at a distance, for both a bird and a human, and besides, it's not one hundred per cent reliable. If you happen to be a bird-ringer and you catch a willow warbler in a mist-net, you should be able to tell it from a chiffchaff because the willow warbler's wings are proportionately longer; a willow warbler flies to Africa for the winter, while a chiffchaff only goes as far as southern Europe, so the willow warbler needs better wings. But a willow warbler is not going to catch another willow warbler in a mist-net, nor is it going to measure its wings with a pair of callipers. So it sings.

The songs of these identical-looking birds are radically different, as we will see when we take a closer listen to both birds later. You don't need to see the bird. A birdwatcher need not watch a willow warbler or a chiffchaff. You only need to listen. If you are a birdlistener you can tell instantly, and with your eyes closed. Willow warblers and chiffchaffs are birdlisteners: so will you be, if you wish.

We humans are different from most mammals. Most mammals have a highly developed sense of smell. For a dog, a lamp-post is a thrilling thing. To a human, a well-sprayed lamp-post is merely mildly disgusting, and a dog's fascination mildly amusing or mildly irritating. But to a dog, it is *The Times* hot off the presses; latest news, social column, gossip. He reads it through his nose and learns which dog passed by when. Then, as if joining an internet chatroom, he will add his own contribution by means of a cocked leg. If you study mammals, you come to understand that an awful lot of the most important matters of their lives are based around urination and defecation: middens, the spraying and scattering of dung. It is impossible for humans to empathise with this: we just don't have the equipment. Our noses are pretty coarse and feeble instruments. We smell in black and white, while a dog smells in eternal rainbows of subtle and delicate nuances. But birds are not great smellers, on the whole. Some vultures use smell to locate carrion; albatrosses can find feeding fish by smell; nightjars and swifts have a reliable sense of smell. But smell is not all and everything to any birds, as it is for a dog. They have other ways of communicating. As a dog pisses, a bird sings.

And a bird's song does something that a pile of dung can never do: it touches a human heart. I have established the presence of otters in front of my house, not, alas, because I have seen their sinuous selves, nor because I have heard their sweet song. No: instead of singing, otters will leave a spraint in a prominent place. Under a bridge is a favourite. A spraint is an otter turd. I rejoice to find a spraint: coiled and fish-stinky under the bridge's arch: but I am not moved by the spraint itself, only by what the spraint means. A spraint touches an otter's heart, but not mine. Like birds, we humans are creatures of sight and sound. Birds bring colour to our eyes: but the brightest and most brilliant thing they possess they bring to us by means of their voices. And like the birds themselves, we humans are touched and moved by birdsong.

Learning birdsong is not just a way to become a better bird-spotter. It is tuning in: a way of hearing the soundtrack of the planet earth.

Robin

Birds sing in spring, so obviously the best time to get started is winter. Birds mostly sing because they are establishing or protecting a territory, and attracting or safeguarding a mate. In other words, most singers are male, they mostly sing about breeding, and breeding is what happens in the spring.

So at the height of spring, a rich chunk of woodland or even a suburban back garden is a glorious cacophony of song. At dawn, every cock bird with aspirations of siring a brood will lift his voice in song. And the dawn chorus at the height of spring is wonderful and it lifts your heart and yes, it's perfectly possible to get a grasp of what's going on and who's singing what to whom – but it's an awfully difficult place to start. If you want to learn the individual instruments of the orchestra, it's probably best not to start with the last movement of Beethoven's Ninth. But it's a fact that learning the instruments will give you a better grasp, a deeper under-standing, a more profound joy in the "Ode to Joy".

Best to start by listening to a few soloists. So listen out on a winter's day: in a garden or a park or a patch of woodland. Choose a stillish calmish brightish day

and the chances are you will hear your
robin. It's a robin, because it's the
only bird that sings consistently
throughout the winter. In fact,
it sings most of the year,
while the rest shut
up once the business
of breeding is over.
Robins, like most birds,
go quiet in the high summer, when
they are moulting and vulnerable and
the last thing they want to do is draw
attention to themselves. But as autumn begins, robins
start to take up territories again. Males and females
will both sing and defend the territories in which they
feed.

When the spring comes around again, robins will
pair up and then defend a breeding territory, quite often
with the same mate as the previous year. The song
continues more or less seamlessly from winter into
spring. At these times, the robins are often the first birds
to sing in the day, and the last ones to stop as it gets
dark.

Listen, then, to the song of the robin. You can do
this by choosing the winter's day; otherwise by listening
to the podcast. The best way to learn is by listening.
It's hard to write the sound of a cello, or to describe
the Bach cello suites, but there is a part of our brain in
which we store the memories of sounds without need

of verbal classification. You can activate this only by listening. First you listen with your conscious mind, but then, soon enough, you will find that the lessons have got embedded. Soon enough, you find that you know you are hearing a robin without needing to think about it. The song has become part of you.

Now here's a complication. The robin doesn't have a single song. But don't get disheartened. A robin loves variations and has a good repertoire, but the tone is the thing. You can use a violin to play Bach or an Irish reel, but it still sounds like a violin. A robin always sounds like a robin: a gentle, pretty, rather thin sort of song. When I was first learning birdsong, I thought of a robin's thin, soft, insect-eater's beak. It goes with a thin, soft song.

Robins are frequently aggressive. The red breast is a token of strength. A robin will flash his breast – a display – towards another red-breasted robin; at peak times he will display at anything red. Robins will frequently follow up a display with an attack, if they come across a rival reluctant to back down. But the song doesn't seem at all warlike to our ears. It seems sweet, and a trifle melancholy. Some say the song gets more melancholy as the year passes into winter.

Listen to your robin. Listen again and again. It's a revision test you can do throughout the winter: every time you hear a bird sing, pause for a moment and listen. And you will learn your robin, and you will begin to notice that every now and then, you hear a bit of song that is not a robin. You are telling one bird from another by means of song. You are tuning in.

Be ecstatic.

Double figures

Are you beginning to get the hang of the robin's song? If so, you may congratulate yourself. You are practically into double figures. You can now recognise getting on for ten birds from the sounds that they make. It's a fact that if you find yourself taking up an interest in any subject, you usually discover that you have been subtly learning it for years, by some kind of unconscious process.

To categorise is a basic human instinct. We do so in order to understand the world. We break things down and place them in the right box. We don't simply accept that some birds have a red breast and others do not: we separate the red-breasted ones and call them robins, and thereby, a rough-and-ready understanding of birds can begin. This is not something that only experts do: we all need to sort things into categories. If something attracts your interest – say, pop music, or films, or cars – then naturally, you start sorting them into finer and finer categories: that's not a folk-song, it's early Dylan; that's not a film with subtitles, it's Fellini; that's not an old sports car, it's an AC Cobra. For most people, a swan is a swan: end of categorisation. But for a birder, it matters that there are three species of swan in Britain and four more worldwide.

Naturally, we do this categorising with sounds as well as sights. We know that this sound is a trumpet, and it's a musical instrument; we know that this sound is a road drill and a machine; and that this sound is a dog barking, a living non-human animal. As a result of that tendency, we can all name a few birds from the sounds they make, without need of learning.

Let's start with a duck. You don't need me to tell you that a duck goes quack. (If you get the hang of birdlistening, you will also come across ducks that whistle and ducks that make a noise like Frankie Howerd looking through a keyhole, but that's by the by.) The most nature-deaf person on the planet will hear a quack and know it is a duck. Most domestic ducks, Aylesburys and Indian runners and so forth, have been selectively bred from mallards, and it's as mallards that they quack. The equation quack-equals-duck is a common experience more or less across the world.

A crow goes caw. The very name suggests the sound: many bird names turn out to be onomatopoeias. Middle English and Old English will give you *crawe*, the Dutch *kraai*, the German *krahe*. The ancient names were probably applied indifferently to carrion crows and rooks, both being large black species of crow. (There are finer categories of crow; in the wild world there are finer categories of practically everything.) The murmuring caws of a rookery in a country churchyard; the angry-sounding triple caw of carrion crow: hear these and you know – you knew already – that you're listening to some kind of crow.

We all know the sound an owl makes. Well, we are all familiar with the long, wavering hoot that you hear in a graveyard at night in a horror film. There are three species of owl you are really quite likely to hear, if you go to the countryside in this country, but never mind the smaller categories for now. If you hear a spooky, if rather stagey woo-ooo-ooo coming out of pitch darkness, you know you have an owl. A tawny owl, if you wish to be more precise.

A seagull makes a series of repeated screams; you hear it on *Desert Island Discs*. Hear the sound on any television programme and you know, faster than you could tell it, that you're at the seaside. These are herring gulls, and they have a decent range of sounds, but this is that characteristic one.

A pigeon coos. There are several species of pigeon and dove in this country, and they all make different sounds, but it is all based on the principle of cooing. Later on I will encourage you to tell one coo from another: but we all know what cooing means.

I heard about a survey in which young people were unable even to hazard a guess at the sound a cuckoo makes. This is not only because we are losing touch with the wild world: we are also losing cuckoos. These birds are much scarcer than they once were, but surely most people are aware that when they hear the sound "cuckoo" they are listening to a cuckoo.

And one more: woodpecker. You hear a sudden brief frenzied machine-gun rattle from the heart of a stand of trees, and you know it's a woodpecker. You may feel that this doesn't count: the bird is not singing but bashing its beak into a dead branch. It's all one to the woodpeckers. They are not looking for food when they drum; they are making a territorial signal. They are percussionists rather than vocalists, but they still send out a loud message in sound, and we humans can pick it up. It's probably a great spotted woodpecker, but again, we'll separate one species from another later on. In the meantime, you already know what a woodpecker sounds like.

So no, you are not nature-deaf. No one is. You are already more tuned in than you thought. If you've got that robin, you can already do eight different kinds of bird with your eyes closed. And you probably know the laid-back song of the blackbird, the screaming of a party of swifts, and when you hear the never-ending song that pours and pelts from the heights, you know it's a skylark.

Deep into double figures.

A place of my own

Territory. Birds sing to protect it. It seems rather a base reason to burst into song, one that debases the entire notion of heart-lifting beauty and so forth. But we mustn't think of territory in human terms – that is to say, ownership. Territory is not property. Nor is singing the avian equivalent of the traditional country greeting: what the fuck are you doing on my land?

Territory is life. Nothing less. It is a bit of space without which a bird could not make more birds: a bit of space that a bird will – must – defend. Your average songbird has a three-tier system of defence, and the first of these is song. If the threat continues, the second level of protection comes in: display. A robin, as you already know, flaunts its red breast. Many species will pose with the head down and the beak held out; others will point the beak skywards and show off the breast. The meaning is clear, or supposed to be: don't bother fighting with *me*. You'd only get yourself into trouble. The whole idea of singing and displaying is not to get into a fight; it is to avoid fighting. But battle is, of course, the third tier, with home advantage being very important.

Territory is a variable thing. For many seabirds, the

idea of a protected space is reduced to a square foot or two: the actual nest site. No bird claims a personal patch of ocean. Such a thing would be meaningless, because shoals of fish move about. It's the exact opposite for a tawny owl: a territory, once established, is likely to serve the bird for the rest of its life.

Many songbirds will set up a seasonal territory, in which they both nest and feed. The size varies a good deal: if there is a lot of food, the birds can be closer together without too much trespassing or stress. Warblers tend to have a fuzzier notion of territory and will defend the place where they happen to be feeding at the time.

But when a bird is singing to protect a territory, it tends to mean that the territory is big enough to need an audible message to cover it all, and that there are enough birds of the same species around to defend it from. The rivals will be birds of the same species. Different species tend not to be in direct competition for the same resources: a blue tit looks for caterpillars on the far ends of branches; a great tit looks for bigger stuff in the middle of trees; a blackbird forages on the ground. The blackbird is worried about other blackbirds; the tits, whether great or blue, don't bother him in the slightest.

Song works. Pure song is often enough to keep the territory safe. One experiment showed that if you take the great tits away from their territory but continue to play the cock's song though loudspeakers, you will keep the territory safe from invasion by other great tits.

Territory is about food, about attracting and keeping a mate, about protection from predators. Ultimately, it's about making more birds: of passing on, as Richard Dawkins would prefer me to say, the bird's immortal genes.

Territory matters. But it is not about showing off, about possession, about my place is bigger than yours. Territory is life, and it follows that the song used to defend a territory is the song of life. We are humans, from the order of mammals; they are birds in the order of Aves. But we, like the birds, respond very strongly to sound. When we hear the song of life, it matters to *us*. We respond, with our guts and with our emotions, to the song that stirs the passions of the listeners of the same species: a song that inspires rivalry and respect and even fear in the male listeners – if the song is good enough. It also inspires desire in the females – again, if the song is good enough. For birds, like humans, are discerning listeners.

Wren

It's a fine winter day. There's not much warmth in the sun, but at least there are shadows on the ground. You're in a good temper: this is a winter's day that promises winter's end. You hear a robin, in good voice, responding to the weather just as you are. And then there's another song. Astonishingly loud, and coming from about knee-high.

That's a wren. A fast volley of alternating notes. More often than not, it's followed by a loud, almost a violent trill. Try rattling your tongue just behind your teeth, as if you were imitating a road drill; that gives a general idea. This is one of the smallest birds in Britain; you could hold a dozen or more in your cupped hands, but when they sing, they really let rip. If you ever see a wren singing, with his cocky tail aloft, you wonder that he doesn't rip himself apart with the effort he pours into his song, body and wings trembling.

That trill at the end of the verse is the thing to hold onto. Once you have got it, it is quite unmistakable. The snag is that a wren won't give you the trill every single time, and is more likely to leave it out in the winter, when he's not seriously involved in setting up a territory: rather, he's preparing for an early start and responding to the promise in the air.

So when you hear a loud and strident burst of winter song, and you know it's not a robin, take a pause and listen. He'll probably put in his trill before long, and then you'll know exactly where you are. After that, you'll start to pick up wren from the initial phrases: as much from the context as anything else. Low down, loud: wren.

As you listen to the wren and get him logged in your brain, you'll find the song – well, a bit samey. Not something that bowls you over with its beauty. A few of those oscillating notes, and then the trill – and, er, that's it. Mechanical, repetitive, unimaginative. But there's a very great mystery attached to this brief explosion of song.

If you record a wren's song, play it back and slow it down, it becomes startlingly different, and a great deal more complex. The slowing-down of birdsong has become rather a thing among ornithologists in recent years: as it were, putting a song under a microscope. And you find that there is a very great deal more to a song that you thought, than you were capable of hearing. I have listened to a burst of song from a wren that lasted 8.25 seconds, slowed down to last for 66 seconds. The transformation is startling: hidden in the hurry is a sweet and leisurely melodic pattern. The wren sang an unbelievable 103 notes in the course of the song: that is to say, he was singing at a speed of 740 notes a minute. Impossible for a human to rival that: impossible, for that matter, for a human to distinguish the individual sounds. Our ears are not that fine.

Does a bird distinguish the individual notes? We can do slightly better than merely saying, presumably, or what would be the point of pouring out all those notes? The whip-poor-will is an American bird, and it is famous for the far-carrying three-note call from which it gets its name. But if you slow it down, you find that the bird is actually singing five notes.

The mocking-bird is a great mimic of all kinds of birdsong, and one of its favourites is the whip-poor-will. Slow down the mocking-bird's imitation of a whip-poor-will and what do you find? Five notes. It seems that to understand and appreciate a bird's song to the maximum, you need to be a bird. Birdsong is more complex and more beautiful than we are capable of understanding: but we can do our best.

Talking birds

When is a song not a song? When it's a call. Birds make noises for reasons other than holding a territory and winning a mate. And to make things more interesting, a lot of birds make a sound to advertise their territory – but not always one that we consider musical, not one we would really call a song. The cock-a-doodle-do of domestic poultry, or if you prefer, of the red jungle-fowl, its wild ancestor, is not in the nightingale class – or even the wren class – as a musical performance.

The notion of song is something that we tend to restrict to – well, songbirds. That is to say, the passerines who establish territories by means of musical and complex vocalisations. This is fair enough, but hardly precise. Passerines, by the way, are perching birds. This is a huge group that includes crows, with magpies and ravens and all. There is a sub group within, sometimes called oscines. This covers all the birds with a complex vocal apparatus that enables them to make complex noises. Or songs. There are about 4,000 species worldwide in this group, from a total of around 10,000 species of bird.

Song, then, is pretty popular, and pretty important. But most birds, oscines or not, make noises; quack-quack, for example. And all songbirds make noises that are not songs. Walk through a wood, or a park, outside the breeding season, when the place is not echoing with song. You will still hear the sound of birds. You may well hear both robin and wren, even if they are not singing. A robin gives a soft click of an alarm call; a wren gives a much louder and more explosive click.

A call is usually very short, often just a single note. A call can be used for a number of different reasons: to keep in touch with other members of a flock; to scold intruders; to encourage others to do the same; to give a warning of danger, if there's a sparrowhawk, say, or a human about; as a threat; to ask for food; to express excitement.

But here's an intriguing thing: these calls are not hard-and-fast categories. It's not a simple matter. The notion of danger doesn't elicit one single response, like a dashboard light coming on when you are running low on oil. The bird's response will indicate the degree of danger, and even the nature of the danger. Obviously, this is useful to other species of bird that are vulnerable to the same kind of danger. Song is always a message to members of the same species; call can be a sharing of information between species.

The calls can be repeated, sometimes very rapidly, and with different levels of intensity. The alarm calls of the mistle thrush, when a magpie makes a dart for the nest, create a vivid drama in which the calls of the mistle thrush escalate rapidly from alarm to berserker fury. As with song, call can also arouse empathy in humans, not so much as a matter of anthropomorphism, sentimental identification with an animal, as the atavistic fellow-feeling of a creature that is, like humans used to be, prey.

Call, then, is a simpler sound than the full song, as we understand it, as sung by most songbirds. But it is a more complex concept. Call can serve many functions. It is subtle, nuanced and variable.

Hard-and-fast criteria are not always helpful. For example, there are times when communication by means of call seems to overlap into communication by means of song, when calling acquires a complexity and a territorial function. There is an overlap, a grey area between song and call. There is also a grey area between the silence of an amoeba and *The Divine Comedy*: a grey area between fully evolved language as we understand it, and nothing. Birds communicate. Often they do so by means of a song that we humans also find interesting and pleasing and even meaningful. They also communicate by means of call, when important concepts can be expressed. That's communication.

So when we listen to the sounds of birds, we are not just indulging our aesthetic sense, or enjoying being aural train-spotters. We are also asking questions about the nature of language, the meaning of sound, the things we have in common with our fellow animals

and our sense of continuity with the non-human world.
And as James Joyce once asked his friend Frank Budgen:
"How's that for high?"

Pee-oo!

A robin makes a clicking call; so does a wren. A robin, one field guide tells you, says "tic" while a wren goes "chek". This is as helpful as you can get, given the obvious limitations of written language. The two calls are quite easy to tell apart once you've got the hang of them – but it is quite impossible to transcribe them so that a reader can tell them apart the first time off. Phonetic transcriptions can be a help: but they can also be confusing. I always like the green pigeon, an African species that, apparently, says "tweeu, tweety, tweety tweety, krrr, krrr, krrup, krrr, kree etc". I love the etc. A field guide has little option but to do the best it can with transcriptions but recordings are much more helpful. So, please use the ones we've put together for this book.

I'm going to avoid these transcriptions as far as possible, since you will have the luxury of listening to recordings, and because I hope you will listen to the actual birds. Look elsewhere, then, for a harsh "kwarr" and short "kwup".

If you feel you are missing out, then blame Bill Oddie. In his delightful *Little Black Bird Book*, he had great fun with transcriptions. He notes: "You'll find roughly a *dozen* different species that are supposed to go 'Pee-oo'. These include little-ringed plover, pygmy owl, short-toed lark, wood warbler, ring ouzel, willow tit and snow bunting – so that's seven different *families*, let alone species!" Oddie accompanies this observation with a charming drawing of seven species forming a kind of choir, all of them singing, "Pee-oo!"

Outside in the real world, the birds don't sound even remotely similar.

How to see round corners

We are aware of the pollution of our senses only by the absence of pollution. We talk about light pollution: but it is a concept we can only understand on a frosty night in the countryside, when we can look up and see a sky full of stars. Or better still, a night in the desert. I remember sleeping out in the Namib Desert. The only light for miles around was the fire. It was a moonless night, not even the moon was there to pollute, and so the sky was white, not black. I seemed to be staring up at every star in the universe.

In town we accept this without giving it much of a thought: a low ceiling created by the artificial lights, from which, on cloudless nights, the moon shines through; sometimes, low on the horizon, the odd planet; exceptionally, a visible constellation.

And it's the same with sound. We are used to the hum of traffic. It's not easy, in lowland Britain, to get away from it. Mostly, we filter it out, as we do ambient music in a pub (until, of course, they play your song). The constant white noise of civilisation creates a drone in our ears. To move away from it – to visit a place where there are no engines for miles – is a shattering experience. When the background drone is silenced, the ear awakes. Try sitting on the banks of the Luangwa River in Zambia, a thing I have done many times. Try lying there in the dark, in your bed, or sitting around the fire when the talk dies down. You hear only the natural sounds, and behind them, the silence that is the absence of humankind. The tinkle of painted reed frogs. The stridulations of the crickets. The dirty guffaw of hippos in the river; the sudden splash as one of their number returns to the waters from a night's grazing. The crump of lion. The whoop of hyena. A sudden uproar in a troop of resting baboons: suddenly all of them awake because there's a leopard about.

And the sound of birds, too, of course. Mozambique nightjar, churring with many gear changes. The grunt of giant eagle owl. The proop of scops owl. The soft repetitions of barred owlet; the more complex whistling hoots of pearl-spotted owlet. The Cape turtle doves: do they never sleep? And the wood owl: now then, *whoooo's* a naughty boy?

Was it on those banks that I really tuned into bird-song, to the sounds of the wild? Was it because out there you need your ears to construct the world? In these places, places where a human can still walk and feel like prey – and for the best of all possible reasons – you need your ears. With your ears you can see round corners. With your ears you can penetrate the eight-foot-high grasses and the thick bush. With your ears you can see in the dark. With your ears, you stay alive.

With your ears – even while walking through a park in central London – you can shake off at least some of your civilised self. With your ears, you can feel yourself more truly what you are: part of the great community of life on earth.

Dunnock

Another singer on that fine winter's day. It's not a robin, because you know that one; it's not a wren because there's no trill and it's not loud enough. It's a short jumble of notes, thrown together in a hurry: a rather flat little burble. Sometimes just a single fragment; sometimes you get one chunk – one verse, if you like – after another, with a pause for thought in between.

This is dunnock. If you were going to be harsh, you could say it was a drab little bird with a drab little song. You'll hear it from hedges and bushes: dunnocks are not as determined low-lifers as wrens, but they are still likely to be found below head-height. They eschew gaudiness in all its forms, but you can, if you prefer, regard them as birds of elegant understatement. Their plumage is a careful mix of blacks and greys and browns; their song is much the same.

A male can have as many as eight different songs, so there's a challenge for a discerning ear. The sound is cheering, jaunty even, and there are times in the early spring when the dunnock is the only singer in full voice, and then he rejoices in the glory of the soloist – before the cacophony grows about him day by day and he is relegated once more to the background.

I should mention, however, that the dunnock is gaudy in one matter, not that you'd think him – or for that matter, her – capable of such things from the drab appearance. Always watch the quiet ones: dunnocks are mad for sex, and multiple infidelities and deceptions mark their lives. The male not only sings and mates, he also goes in for cloacal pecking, in which he attempts to remove any sperm deposited by a previous male. The hedges of Britain are a hotbed of passion. But that is what singing is all about.

Time and space

Now here's a rum thing: you don't often hear a duck in the middle of an oakwood. The chances of hearing a raven in your back garden are slight. And you probably won't hear a robin singing in the middle of Brighton beach either. This is something that matters very much, and for two separate reasons. The first is your personal convenience as a birdlistener. The second is more to do with the meaning of life – so we'd better get the convenience reason out of the way first.

To be a birder – to be a naturalist of any kind – is pretty simple. You just have to become a master of time and space. Birds sing as flowers bloom and as butterflies fly: at particular times and in particular places. In order to recognise and begin to understand the birds, you need to recognise and understand the times and the places. And that works the other way round as well, creating a rather pleasingly virtuous circle, in which each visit to a place adds to your understanding of its birds, and each acknowledgment of a bird adds to your understanding of its place. That principle works with time as well: time of day, season of the year.

Birds, like, most living things, have a context. I remember completely failing to recognise the call of a dunnock. I thought it was an unfamiliar sandpiper, and scanned the shoreline eagerly. My mind was all on waders and other birds of the shore, because I was in north Norfolk waiting for the tide to bring the waders in. The dunnock called from a few scrappy bushes behind the hide I was roosting in. It threw me, because the bird was out of context, or at least, seemed so. I had forgotten about the bushes in my eagerness for the birds of the shore.

Recognising a bird sound from no context whatsoever is very hard. I have been caught out more than once, generally on the radio when they have played me a chunk of bird sound and challenged me to identify it. The mind goes blank: are we in the garden sipping Pimms in late spring, or on an open boat offshore in the depths of winter? I have failed these tests ignominiously.

The human mind demands context, not just for the convenience of identification, but in order to understand what the whole thing is about. You are not, in the normal course of events, going to hear a kittiwake in Birmingham or a woodpecker on the rocks at Land's End.

And so, as you tune into birds, you tune into places. Robin, wren, dunnock – you will find these in gardens, in parks, in the suburbs, in woodland. They are happy to live on the fringes of human life. That, in a country massively modified by humans, is their context, and the secret of their success.

Other birds require different places. That's because they live in different ways. That are as many species of bird as there are ways in which a bird can make a living on this planet. So as you tell one bird from another, you are not filling up your stamp album or ticking off numbers in your train-spotter's book; you are coming to an understanding about the basic mechanism of life. Life works by making lots and lots of different kinds of living things.

Birds are perfect for helping you to reach this understanding. They not only have their being in colour and sound, they come in the right kind of numbers for humans to grasp. In this country there are a couple of hundred species of bird you might reasonably expect to see; 300 if you get serious about making a list, and 400 if you get obsessive. Perfect. There are more than 23,000 species of insect in this country, which is simply boggling. There are 10,000 species of birds in the world, with the odd one here and there yet to be described. It's just about possible to deal with that figure. There are a million species of insect, with maybe five, maybe ten million more waiting to be described: and each one of them has its own utterly viable evolved way of living – and that's as hard to grasp as the notion of interstellar distances.

So let us concentrate on the sort of numbers our minds can hold without getting dizzy. That is to say, birds. The knowledge of just a few will open the portals of understanding. And as you add a few more, and then a few more, a deeper understanding cannot help but follow. I don't mean understanding as learning a set of plain old facts: I mean understanding in the deep dark intuitive parts of yourself. You can understand a person in one way by reading a CV; you can also understand a person in other, deeper ways by meeting, talking, knowing, enduring, loving. You can do both these things with the wild world.

Birdsong to save your life

Knowledge of birdsong can save your life. I am quite certain that it did so on a daily basis for our ancestors. It is possible that without a knowledge of the sounds of birds, the first humans who walked the African savannahs would have gone extinct, and modern humans would never have happened.

You're walking in thickish bush. You can move all right, there are plenty of paths and gametrails to follow, but you can't see more than a few yards in any one direction. And then you hear a hissing, cackling call. Instantly, you stop, listen, assess, and then either investigate or pick your way round whatever it is that is making the sound.

No, it's not a flock of giant fierce birds that dine on humans. They're oxpeckers. They eat mainly insects. Black birds, rather starling-like, and in fact related, though not very closely, to starlings. The noise they make is a little starling-like, too. They make their living by eating the parasites that attack large mammals. This would make a sweeter and more charming picture of the kindness of nature if the birds didn't also feast on flesh from the open wounds of the animals they sit on. But what matters to the walking human is that if you hear the hiss of oxpeckers, you know that there is likely to be a large mammal ahead of you: perhaps buffalo, a rhino, or a hippo. Animals that can kill a human without very much trouble.

If you are a more advanced student of bird sound, and I think we can assume that our ancestors were, then you can distinguish between the sounds made by the two species of oxpecker. The yellow-billed oxpeckers have a thinner beak, and they work with a stabbing action. The red-billed oxpeckers do this too, but they also work with a scissor action, and so they are better able to work on the hairier mammals, combing through the fur for delicious parasites. This means that red-billed oxpeckers are particularly suited to working on the necks of giraffes, and on animals as small and slender as impalas. As I mentioned a couple of pages back, birds have come up with thousands of different ways of making a living, there being thousands of species of bird. Here are two such methods. Human imagination would have struggled to come up with one single idea: that there was a living to be made from the ecto-parasites and the living flesh of large mammals. The fact that there are two demonstrates the endless virtuosity of the forces of evolution. Two species of oxpecker: two ecological niches: pretty close, and with a substantial area of overlap, but each species quite separate.

This doesn't mean that if you hear red-billed oxpecker

you are automatically safe; the red-bills are perfectly capable of feeding on the less-hairy mammals. But if you hear yellow-bills, you know that the chances of this being a dangerous mammal – a buffalo, a hippo – are higher. Our ancestors knew how to play the percentages. Birdsong is the sound of life, the music of life and the meaning of life: it is also a matter of life and – well, death.

Long-tailed tit

Life goes on, even in winter. It has to. There's not so much food around, the weather is cold and to withstand cold you need energy. So for a bird, the few brief daylight hours of winter are a frenzied search for food: sufficient unto the day: enough to get you a day closer to the spring. Birds don't sleep the winter out like hedgehogs, bats and a few butterflies: their high metabolism requires constant topping up. For birds, the winter is about hanging on, getting through, keeping safe. In the long darkness the songbirds roost and then, in the short day, they try and fill themselves up with enough food to get through the night. Plenty don't make it. There are always more birds going into the autumn than there are birds going into the spring.

Take a winter walk though a copse, or in a park, along a hedgerow, or an avenue – anywhere where there are trees reasonably close together. Most probably, you won't be aware of any birds at all – and then suddenly you are aware of a lot. You have come across a party of long-tailed tits.

These joyous little birds have their being in togetherness. They hate to be alone. They don't feel complete

unless they
are a dozen or so,
sometimes even more, and in
the silent months they are terribly
obvious, because they yell. All the
time. As they travel together, so they
keep in the closest possible touch with
each other. And they do so by yelling at
each other. I'm *here* – where are you? I'm here – where
are *you*? They do all this with a frantic call. *Sisisi! Sisisi!*
(I apologise if this a bit of a pee-oo moment.) It's not
a song: it's a contact call. With long-tailed tits it's an
expression of unity. Contact is what they love above all
else.

You will hear them above your head, or across the
road, or the far side of the field. You will catch glimpses
of them: sometimes they make the mad transition from
tree to tree all together, sometimes in threes and fours,
sometimes in line astern. They are tiny things, and their
stick-and-ball shape is very distinctive – but you have
already recognised them by their call, by the perpetual
busy-ness implied by the din of the passage.

They will make three or four notes when they call to
each other, a sequence that travels a little way down the
scale. When extra-excited – and they are excitable little
birds – they will trill and burr the calls, and this burring
can easily escalate to a full alarm call. They watch

out for each other, these long-tailed tits, like arboreal meerkats.

If you stop to take a look at a party of long-tailies, you will often find other species among them: a mixed flock of busy little birds working the trees, forming a temporary alliance as they get through the next bit of winter. To be part of a bird party is safer than being on your own, and besides, you can often find food in the disturbance a large party makes as it travels. And as the long-tailed tits constantly call, other species can take advantage of their safety-in-numbers policy. The long-tailies have been called the convenors of the flock: birds who seem to have taken on the job of leading the littlest songbirds towards the long-in-coming spring.

First Spring

First Spring

How to make spring
last longer

Did you ever wish that spring lasted longer? Did you ever wish that spring started earlier – at the end of January, for example? Well, now it does. Tune into bird-song and you tune into the real, the deep patterns of the seasons. The first day of spring isn't the day you leave off your overcoat, it began long before that.

Spring doesn't begin with a sudden explosion of song. The birds don't all start at once, in a single great joyous bellow, like the *Sanctus* in the B Minor Mass. It's more a steady trickle. One voice at a time, one species at a time. It's a process that has many setbacks: a fine evening will bring in two, three new singers, but when the cold, wet wintry morning follows, they will shut up again.

It's not smooth and continuous, but once the process has started, there is no going back. Even if they go quiet again for a bit, a Rubicon has been crossed, and winter's conquest has begun. That's the tremendously heartening thing about birdsong: it tells you, even in the midst of what looks like winter's triumph, that spring is on the move.

We are all affected by the lack of sunlight in winter, some more than others. Winter blues, or Seasonal Affective Disorder, is part of the human condition for those of us who live with the passage of the seasons. That has to be the case, or we wouldn't feel joy in the coming of spring. And for years, my own tendency to gloom in the darker months has been appreciably helped by the most courageous early singers. You can feel it soon after Christmas, as the days get subtly longer and the spring singing begins. It's a sense of a reprieve. Your appeal has been answered, your sentence has been reduced, you've got time off for bad behaviour: soon you'll be free.

As the spring continues, more and more of the resident birds take up a territory and begin to sing. Then, as spring carries on, the migrants begin to arrive. Some come hurriedly; others, having further to travel, take their time. And then there are stragglers who turn up when it seems almost too late. As spring advances, so the population increases, so the diversity of species increases, and so the great rolling crescendo continues towards its Maytime peak.

Spring is a not a single event. I use the word "crescendo" in the stricter sense: not a moment of ultimate loudness or intensity, but a strong, steady increase, one that begins after Christmas and keeps going until about the first week in May, whereupon the diminuendo begins.

One by one the chorus swells, till it's a mighty noise,

as the song by the Incredible String Band tells us: but that's not the story of a single day. It's the story of the march of spring.

Great tit

What is the first song of spring? The first singer of the year? Who has to open the show cold? An impossible question: hard-and-fast boundaries are not a feature of the wild world, for all that such things gratify human minds. For a start, there are plenty of birds singing already, with robin and dunnock and wren, and what's more, there are plenty of calls that have a territorial function. I once heard a woodlark in full song on December 20, letting rip in full song as if he had the sun of April on his back. One of the most spectacular early singers is the mistle thrush, prone to filling the January air with a wonderfully wild and aspirational song – but we'll save him for later. Let us first try and establish some of the basic grammar of the spring.

And that means great tit. There comes a moment in the early spring when, for the first time, you hear a strident, lung-busting two-note call, with a very strong stress on the first syllable. Teacher, teacher, teacher: that's the usual mnemonic, though some people find that confusing. So if you prefer, it's a squeaky pump, with a strong push on the down stroke and an easy recovery stroke.

Once started, the song doesn't seem to stop much: as if it is the great tit's duty to wake up all the other birds and tell them to start singing. It is the first arrow aimed at winter's heart. Once winter hears that two-stroke note, it knows it's a goner. The game is up: winter can prolong itself as hard as it likes, but the great tit's voice says that the endgame has begun – and the singers are going to win it.

The great tit is a gabby bird. It has lots of variations and an astonishingly large repertoire of calls. A loud churr is probably the most obvious, but here's a wonderful thing. As you begin to listen, as you begin to tune in, you can begin to recognise birds, particularly in the shorter calls, just from the tone and the context. In the same way that a cricketer gets his eye in after he's batted a few overs, so as a birder, you will get your ear in. Hmm, you say – that sounds like a great tit. And it probably is. And if it then makes a churr or makes its twin-syllable song, or hops into view, you know you're right and you've just increased your own repertoire.

But I'd better finish with another thought from Bill Oddie. The great tit is famous, even notorious, for its large vocabulary: "One final piece of advice from years of experience – if you hear a call and don't recognise it – it's a great tit."

51

Keeping it simple

Once the great tit starts to sing, it begins to get complicated. More and more birds join in. Some of these – blue tits and coal tits, for example – have been putting in odd fragments of song throughout the winter. But once the teacher-teacher song begins, they start to get more vocal as well. They are responding to the changes in the year rather than each other, but I imagine there is a knock-on effect from the actual singing as well, one that works across the boundaries of species.

So here's the plan. I want you to keep going. I really don't want you to get bogged down at this very early stage – so let's save a good few of these birds till later. For your first spring as a birdlistener, I want you to concentrate on the big, important and unmistakable songs. Later on, I'll take you into your second spring, when you can expand your range and take on some more difficult birds. Let's pass on for the moment, leaving you with the thought that up in the higher branches, in the canopies of copses, you will hear a murmuring and churring; some of it's great tit, and some of it sounds a bit like great tit but doesn't seem quite right, and that's probably other members of the tit family. Be happy to leave it like that for now, for as spring advances, one of the finest singers of all is ready to make his entrance.

But before we go on, I should make a point about all those tits. There was a time when, as I emailed my wildlife column for *The Times*, it regularly failed to arrive, and we had to resort to devious methods of squeezing it into the *Times* system. Eventually we discovered what was wrong. There is a firewall around the system, and all material to do with betting and pornography is automatically shut out. As a result, every time I wrote about tits, the column was deemed obscene and therefore wasn't accepted by the system.

The techies managed to work their way around the problem. But I can't help feeling that *The Times* system was right. The birds are singing about sex. Well, what else would they be singing about? So let's move on to one of the most sexy singers you will ever listen to.

Song thrush

Careless rapture. That's what the song thrush specialises in. It's a phrase familiar to us all, but it was coined for a song thrush. Robert Browning was the man, the poem is "Home Thoughts From Abroad", the one that begins "Oh, to be in England/Now that April's here." Browning, clearly a decent birder, takes us through chaffinch and whitethroat before telling us:

> That's the wise thrush; he sings each song twice over
> Lest you should think he never could recapture
> The first fine careless rapture!

The phrase is used these days for such things as one-sight stands, but the thrush is looking for a more permanent arrangement, one that will last through to the summer, and will involve the vital joint enterprise of making more song thrushes.

And at the heart of the song thrush song is repetition. Singing it twice over, or thrice, or even more. The singing male picks on a phrase, and performs a series of repetitions. A brief pause to regroup and then another phrase. And again one more: a set of repetitions often concluded by a more whimsical cluster of warbling, often with some harsher, advanced and challenging material involved. But listen out for a bird that is incredibly loud and given to repeating phrases, and you have found a song thrush. Gardens, parks, farmland: anywhere there is a good mixture of trees to perch on and open land to forage on.

Song thrushes respond to the lengthening hours of daylight. I have often heard them singing by artificial light. I remember hearing one in Soho Square long after respectable citizens had gone to bed. It's my belief that the nightingale that sang in Berkeley Square was a song thrush. (It certainly wasn't a nightingale – they've never been urban, or even suburban birds.)

As you start to listen to a song thrush, you will notice

that he comes up with a good number of different phrases to repeat. He seems sometimes to be making rather a point of the numbers of different phrases he can come up with. And as you listen, you will begin to notice some familiar sounds mixed in among the purely musical phrases. There is, for example, a bird near me who sings like a reversing van. There's a tractor yard on the other side of the street, and vans are always backing in there. Some vans play a little tune when they do so, as a warning. The song thrush picked this up, learned it, and incorporated it into his repertoire.

The song thrush will also bring in the songs and calls of other species of bird: the piercing referee's-whistle sound of nuthatch is a particular favourite. I often hear a song thrush doing a bit of green woodpecker and tawny owl, also redshank. The mimicry is not necessarily slavish, either: the bird seems to have a musical imagination and will use a sound he has heard as a basis for a musical phrase. An improvisation, if you like, like a jazz musician.

Quite obviously, then, this is not just a hard-wired response. Descartes said that all animals, being unable to think, were simply automata, like clocks. But the song thrush seems to be a conscious musician. He isn't born with the ability to produce a single signal that means "this is my place, males keep off, females welcome any time". Rather, he acquires songs throughout his life, polishes and refines them, and produces them as an individual performance: original, yet clearly part of the song thrush genre. This isn't just a business of stimulus and response: extra light, perform a song, you hit my knee and my knee jerks. There is something of composition here, a sense not just of species but of individuality.

Why?

Get a load of that repertoire

The better the song, the sexier the singer. Females are attracted to the males with the biggest repertoires of songs. That is true of a great tit, which might have half a dozen songs in his repertoire; it is true of a song thrush, who may have more than 200; it is true of a nightingale, who might have 300; it is true of the brown thrasher of North America, who may have as many as 2,000 songs and is therefore the world champion. That's if you don't count the sedge warbler, who may never sing exactly the same sequence twice in his entire life. Scientists have played recordings of sedge warbler song to female sedge warblers, and they have learned unequivocally that the bigger the repertoire of the male, the more the female will respond by displaying.

This is where the science gets complex and where hard-and-fast facts are not easy to establish. A bigger repertoire indicates an older bird, because the songs need to be learned. (But there's a converse – it has also been shown that with some species, birds with smaller repertoires are unsuccessful and die younger.) An older bird is by definition more experienced; he will have a better territory than a young bird and be more capable of feeding his nestlings. As a survivor himself, he is more likely to leave surviving offspring than a lesser male.

Starlings don't defend a territory, merely the nesthole. But the male is, as we will see, a terrific performer, and a great mimic, a bird that prides himself on a large repertoire – and it has been shown that females, despite the lack of an obvious territorial benefit, will go for the singer with the best repertoire. The implication is that males with a bigger repertoire are a better bet when it comes to raising young successfully.

If you take a great tit away from his territory, it will probably remain uninvaded, at least for a while, if you play great tit song over a speaker, as we have seen. But it has also been demonstrated that the greater the repertoire that comes out of that speaker, the less likely the place is to be invaded, and the longer it is likely to remain safe. Repertoire attracts females: it also repels males.

In other words, the more creative and imaginative the singer, the more successful he is, both in worldly terms – what he gets for himself – and in evolutionary terms – the number of successful descendants he rears. Now here, of course, we are beginning to stray into the terrifying arena of anthropomorphism. If you are a scientist, you will get laughed out of the profession for any hint of so terrible a thing. But I am inclined to wonder if a bird *enjoys* singing.

This is not a scientific question. It is not amenable to proof or disproof, now or at any time in the future, which takes it beyond science's remit. But humans enjoy singing, so why shouldn't a bird? Sure, with a bird, singing is a natural function – but I have enjoyed fulfilling quite a lot of natural functions myself, here and there. Why shouldn't other animals feel enjoyment in such things as food and sex? I remember watching a pair of lions copulate: after they disengaged, the female rolled onto her back and squirmed about in what was almost a parody of lasciviousness. Someone in the vehicle remarked: "She looked like she really enjoyed that." It was a joke, and it got a laugh, but I took it seriously. Why shouldn't lions be given the reward of pleasure for pursuing their evolutionary destiny? Lions make a big thing of copulation; one couple was recorded as performing 86 times in 24 hours. We know from domestic life that a dog feels and expresses pleasure, and that a cat does the same, in its own way. I'd be very surprised if the two lions I watched didn't feel really rather good about life.

And I'd be surprised if a song thrush, belting out his repertoire at the top of his voice on a fine spring morning, isn't rewarded for pursuing his evolutionary destiny by a feeling of creativity, joy and fulfilment – and that listening females aren't powerfully moved by the song. The song moves us humans, and we aren't even the same species; we don't even belong in the same class of vertebrates. So how much more must it move the singer and his listeners? A male song thrush puts into his song everything he has learned. It is the song of himself: he *is* the song. It's all and everything, and that's why he gives it everything. And that's what artists do, what *great* artists do.

Chaffinch

Chaffinches are not big on repertoire. They may have as many as half a dozen different songs, but it takes a bit of an ear to separate them. What they do have is tenacity. Once they start singing in early spring, they go at it. It's a song that lasts a couple of seconds. Then they pause for a few seconds and do it again. And again. And again. Several times a minute, and they'll go on for hours. A chaffinch is a lesson on the cost of song: when does it eat? To establish and then hold a territory and a mate is a colossal effort, as you'd find yourself if you tried to sing at the top of your voice all day. It's a very serious test of a bird's strength, which is why it works in evolutionary terms as a demonstration of a male bird's strength – that is to say, his potential as a mate. To sing all day, you've got to be good. It's a process that weeds out the bluffers with ruthless efficiency. Nature doesn't do a lot of ruth.

The song itself is jolly enough. It starts up quite slowly, gets quicker and quicker, and ends in a flourish. It is usually compared to a fast bowler's run-up and delivery: a brief build-up to a decisive conclusion.

Chaffinches also have a good range of calls, one of

which sounds like "finch". They used to say "finch" while hopping across the threshing floor, searching through the chaff for seed: a good name. There is also a call that is a kind of shorthand for song: a monosyllabic call with a territorial meaning. And here's a rum thing: the call varies considerably from place to place. Is this a hard-wired response we have yet to understand? Or is it more simply an aspect of chaffinch culture? I'll leave that one with you.

Saying your own name

There are a good few birds that can say their own names. Chaffinches, as we have seen, say finch, and so they give their name to their entire family, who don't say finch at all. Whooper swans certainly whoop: a far-carrying bugle call. Teals – a small duck – make a sound like "teal" when feeding. Smews, another duck, say smew.

Birds of prey tend not to have sonic names, but the sound of their cry can be found in bijou residences across London. A mews was once a stable-yard, and before that, it specifically meant a place you kept your falcons. And falcons most certainly make mewing calls.

Capercaillie means "horse of the woods", on the rather curious notion that the final part of the court-ship song of the male sounds like a whinnying horse. A corncrake clearly says crake, and can even say its own name in Latin: *Crex crex*. A coot also says its own name. Lapwings are also called pewits, and that's a very good onomatopoeia. Curlews call curlew across the winter salt marshes, and black-tailed godwits say godwit, though bar-tailed godwits don't.

Skua is reckoned to be an onomatopoeia if you go far

enough back, while kittiwakes, ocean-going gulls, call kittiwake with three-syllable pedantry. Cuckoos obviously say cuckoo, and hoopoes not only say hoop-oop-oop, they also say their scientific name, which is *Upupa epops*. Lark is said to come from a semi-onomatopoeic term for song, as in lalala. The woodlark sings its generic name, *Lullula arborea*; the French name is *alouette loulou*. Pipits say pipit. Stonechats make a sound like two stones being knocked together. Thrush comes from an earlier name, throstle, which is onomatopoeic, as you will understand now you have got the hang of the song of the song thrush. Many warblers warble, and a chiffchaff unambiguously says chiffchaff, though German chiffchaffs say *zilpzalp*. Twite and siskin are both onomatopoeias.

The more obvious and the more noisy the bird, the more likely it is to be given an onomatopoeic name. Thus all crows caw, or craw if you prefer; it's more or less the same sound. In Latin they say *Corvus* and they are known collectively as corvids – even though one of their number is the jackdaw, which says jack. The chough, another kind of crow, doesn't say chuff, but instead it says chow, so it's our pronunciation that's wrong rather than the birds. A dove doesn't say dove: rather, it coos. What it says is doooove, so that's another onomatopoeia we pronounce wrong.

All of which goes to show how important birdsound used to be: how it was the first thing people thought of when considering the bird. Birdsound was once a common language for people as well as for birds. The sound of birds was not the preserve of the specialist; it was a right and proper pursuit for human beings: just part of being alive in a living landscape. The idea that birdsong, that birds, that wildlife are a matter only for the enthusiast and the buff would have seemed a madness to the people of a couple of hundred years back, who were as familiar with the birds as we are familiar with the makes of cars and the names of celebrities.

I'm not talking about the sound of birds in general, as a vague background twittering – I'm talking about the sound and the song of individual species of bird as a natural and inevitable and, above all, meaningful part of life. It can be again. Help yourself.

(There is no bird called a pee-oo.)

Blue tit

B lue tits, being great garden birds, are around us all the time, but their song is not blindingly obvious. For a start, it is pretty variable, on a limited scale. There are quite a few birds like that: the best way to learn them is to get one example of the song firmly logged in your mind, and then, when you hear it for real, you will know you have found your bird. After that, you can listen. That way, you will pick up other songs in that bird's repertoire, and also acquaint yourself with the general nature and tone of the bird.

Blue tit song is sweeter and gentler than great tit: less declamatory. If you hear a bird that reminds you – in tone rather than in the song itself – of great tit, but doesn't seem brassy enough, then you have probably picked out a blue tit by default. There's a characteristic phrase that is as easy to remember as it is easy to pick out: two clearly separated syllables followed by two hurried conjoined ones. The bird saying: "I'm – a – blue-tit." As if the bird had decided to get all bombastic on you and then lost its nerve halfway through. Hear that, and then let the blue tit do the hard work of telling you its other songs. There are churring alarm notes that are, again, like a great tit but gentler.

I hope I haven't made the blue tit sound too difficult, but it's at this point of the book that you're going to have to start taking on more of the work yourself. The best birdsong tutors are birds, and the blue tit will tell you more about the blue tit's song than I can. So when you have picked out a blue tit, or for that matter, any other bird, take a moment to listen and absorb. That way the song will get logged more securely in your mind, and then the natural and inevitable variations and the individual touches will also start to come through to you. I am deeply happy to start you on the great adventure of birdsong, but eventually, the birds will take over from me and lead you much further than I could ever take you.

Great spotted woodpecker

There is an unexpected bonus that comes very early in the learning of birdsound, and it is called great spotted woodpecker. It is a fact that once you have tuned in and got your ears working, you will discover that there are far more species than you thought, and so many of them within your reach, just knocking about the same world as you. Very early indeed, you suddenly realise that the world – or at least the tree-filled part of it – is crowded with great spotted woodpeckers.

These are traditionally considered a mild exoticism: a bird that might, if you are really lucky, pay a visit to the bird-feeder. But once you have logged their most characteristic sound in your brain, you will start to find them every day of your life. In both contact and alarm, great spotted woodpeckers make a loud, slightly squeaky pik. The birds are not always easy to see, because they spend a good deal of their time high up in the canopy. You'd think from their colour scheme – loudly marked black and white with strong contrasty red bits – that they would be pretty easy to pick out in any tree, but in fact, the plumage works very effectively at breaking up the bird's outline. It is a classic piece of disruptive camouflage.

But great spotted woodpeckers frequently fly from tree to tree. They don't require a closed-canopy woodland to operate in; they are pretty competent at living in suburbia, in and around gardens and parks, also farmland and hedgerows, anywhere where there are decent trees, even when there are gaps between them. And when they fly, they will often make this pik call: You can catch a glimpse of them: their flight is very distinctive, because they go up and down a lot, swoopy, switchbacky and showing off a shortish tail and serrated wings. Then they hit a tree and slap themselves against the trunk.

Once you have picked up that pik call, you will start hearing greatspots all over the place, and you will realise that they are very successful birds who make a living anywhere there are trees. In spring they use these trees as a drum. The ratatat drumming is nothing to do with feeding: it is a territorial signal. When a greatspot is feeding, you will hear a single thwock every ten seconds or so; when you hear an extended rattle, you are listening to the great spotted woodpecker's music. They choose percussion rather than voice, and it works for them. Lesser spotted woodpeckers also drum: but here's the point: they drum in a different way. The great spotted is stronger and briefer, with fewer strokes, scarcely ever more than 20; the lesserspot is softer and more protracted, with 25 strokes or more. (The volume depends on what they are using as a drum: some branches

– and they will even use metal posts – are more resonant than others.) This is amusing for the birdlistener, and it is essential for the woodpeckers. Birdsound, when it carries a territorial meaning, simply doesn't work if it is ambiguous. Birds have to know whether or not it is their own species making the music, whether in song or percussion.

But the greatspot's pik call is the thing to hang onto, because you will hear it often, and throughout the year, even if all birds live more intensely and are consequently more vocal during the spring. Learn that pik and your life will be full of greatspots.

How we stole the music

Some mammals sing. I have heard the song of black howler monkey *Alouatta pigra* singing its own work and Emma Kirkby singing the work of Johann Sebastian Bach, the last two named both representing *Homo sapiens*. Without wishing to be unkind to the howlers, I'd have to say that when it comes to pure musicality, Emma is my singer of choice. However, when it comes to a musical choice between Emma and a nightingale, the decision is not so straightforward. The music Emma sings is created by humans for humans and is intended to carry direct and complex meanings, so as an artistic experience, she and Johann are probably ahead. But the point is that the nightingale is in there and at least to a degree, competing on the same terms: offering a beauty and excitement and a meaning that is purely musical and which touches the minds, hearts and souls of humans as well as nightingales.

There are a good few non-human mammalian singers: that is to say, mammals that use great far-carrying noises as an important part of their way of attacking life. Lions are pretty good. When a lion gives a proper roar, it is a series of explosive belches, rising in intensity and then fading away, till finally there is nothing more than a mere huff. Old African joke: where is the lion, if you can hear the huff? Answer: too close. And yes, I have heard the huff, in huts at night, in tents, and out in the open, and very wonderful and thrilling it is, too. More thrilling still is the full pride chorus: when the entire pride sings a song of triumph and challenge and territory and mutual satisfaction. They love to use rivers as an amp, and individuals or entire prides will sing in response to each other, song and counter-song echoing and re-echoing along the hollow bed of the stream. It's one of the most thrilling and chilling sounds in the world … but it's not what we humans consider great in terms of music.

I have heard hoolock gibbon singing in their family groups to greet the new day: a great intense whooping to which each member gives absolutely everything. And it is deeply stirring as it travels across the rolling canopy of the rainforest: but again, musically it falls a fair way short of the highest class. Wolves, like lions, are great singers, and will readily respond to a human imitator howling across a valley. Great stuff: but it's probably true to say that in musical terms their Bach is a good deal worse than their bite. The tree hyrax of Africa is an amazing vocalist; its nocturnal territorial song is a great prolonged rhythmic scream. Some rodents sing, notably the disturbingly carnivorous grasshopper mouse.

Even in cities we hear something of mammalian song, in the barking choruses of dogs, especially on those nights when the local dog population start playing the game of who's going to have the last bark. Cats will give out a caterwauling chorus, when rival males compete for a receptive female: cat muezzins calling other cats to prayer, as Anthony Powell once wrote.

Whales really do sing, and the songs of humpback whales express a profound individuality and musicality. Their songs are not very close to human ideas of music, but in terms of complexity and meaning, they may be the most complex piece of non-human music on earth. They do not strike an instant human empathy, however. They are not part of us. Very few humans got to hear the songs before modern recording equipment was developed. Whalesong is fascinating, but it is not a part of the ancient human understanding of the world.

When it comes to land mammals, the only one of us that sings in any musical sense of the term is man. This is not least because we have the physical equipment to make noises that can become song, that can become language. It is likely that song is one of the oldest parts of ourselves: older, perhaps, than language – perhaps even essential to the development of language. And we have very clear ideas about what constitutes a tuneful sound and what does not.

Where did we get this from? I am inclined to believe that we stole it. That we stole music from the birds. Our ancestors listened to the sound of birds and responded to the birds that made the most pleasing sounds. And no doubt imitated them: and no doubt incorporated them into performance – to express individuality; to express togetherness; to impress beautiful women or handsome men as pop stars do today; just for the pleasure (remember lions and sex) of the song itself. As our ancestors walked the savannah, did they choose to imitate the sounds that appealed to them most: the whistles of orange-breasted bush shrike and black-naped oriole; the complex songs of Heuglin's robin and the chorister robin; the duets of the collared barbet; the basso pre-dawn hooting of ground hornbill?

This is, of course wild speculation, nothing to do with science. But the non-human world echoes with music, and the best and easily the most accessible examples of that music come from birds. The human world is full of man-made music: but it came from an original idea of the class of Aves. Birds gave us the chants of our oldest ancestors; birds gave us folk songs; birds, ultimately, gave us Bach.

Blackbird

The most pleasing – as opposed to thrilling or stirring or sparkling – birdsong that you can listen to
is the blackbird's, at least it is in this country. There are
other birds with more dramatic, more complex, more
extraordinary and altogether more challenging songs,
but the blackbird is always sweet and delightful and –
rather deceptively – simple. It is too demeaning to say
that blackbirds specialise in the easy-listening music
of the bird world; it is more accurate to suggest that
the blackbird's song is like great music that has been
given a demeaning role, in the way that baroque music
is used as background music in restaurants, or when
the operator puts you on hold. It's not that *The Four
Seasons* is anything other than a great piece of music;
it's just that we have lost something of the sense of
its greatness by putting it to this use. We have ignored
the deeper and more challenging aspects of the music
and concentrated on its superficial prettiness. It is easy
to do that with the song of the blackbird: the background music to a drink in the garden or a walk in
the park.

Blackbirds whistle. They whistle almost like a man,

leaning dreamily against the wall with his hands in his pockets, not too stressed about his next appointment. Strange to think this most relaxed and easy of songs represents the urgent demands of a cock blackbird's deepest nature. I've heard the song described as *dolce far niente*: the sweet doing of absolutely nothing, the joy of idleness. This is a false interpretation, of course: unambiguously anthropomorphic. To a blackbird, eager to fulfil his biological destiny, his song is as stimulating as a war-trumpet and as explicit a lovesong as "Je t'aime" or "Why Don't We Do It in the Road?"

But we listen as humans, not as blackbirds, and so we savour the easiest part of the song: the sweet whistle that we associate with the lengthening hours of daylight, the returning warmth, the garden and the park bench. The song seems to be a celebration of all that is benign in nature: never mind the fact that it is a matter of life and death to the blackbirds.

Blackbirds sound like flutes, the sweetest and least challenging of all the instruments of the orchestra. They sing something we instantly understand as a melody. They sing in verses, and vary the melody with each verse. No human ear can mistake this for anything other than music; no human ear can fail to find it beautiful.

When you actively listen to blackbirds, as opposed to enjoying them as background music, they become a great deal more complex and difficult. Each verse is likely to be concluded with edgier, more rapid notes – rasping, grating, far more demanding that you first thought. Tune into these and you find a musician with a greater range than you expected, one that, apparently, is prepared to shock as well as please. They begin their song later in the year than song thrushes, and they seem to celebrate not the anticipation but the achievement of spring. For them, the delayed moment of reaching full song is a very serious thing.

But before this big decision has been taken, they test themselves over the colder months, frequently ending each day with what is usually called a "chinking chorus". In the dusk, a blackbird will announce his location with a chink; neighbouring blackbirds will respond the same way. The night is brought in with this understated and unmelodic chorus, which is not explicitly territorial, but which has some kind of territorial implication.

Most people will be familiar enough with the blackbird alarm call, even if they haven't specifically logged it as such. The sudden noisy rattle as a blackbird retreats when you step unexpectedly into the garden is part of the texture of suburban life.

Blackbirds are bringers of music. More obviously than any other bird, they bring birdmusic to humans, because they are intensely musical birds who are very happy to live their lives around humans. Blackbirds have defined, and perhaps in part created, our idea of birdsong, and they have contributed vastly to the way we understand it. This understanding is, as I say, slightly warped, because we hear the song as something purely beautiful, something obviously benign. There is a struggle for existence in every ambiguous line of the sweet and dreamy blackbird melody.

When the singing began

If I want to show that humans learned music from the singing of birds, then obviously I have to show that songbirds were around before humans started singing and making music. That's not a problem. The world was full of birdsong long before there were humans to listen to it. Humans – in any modern and recognisable sense of the term – have been around for 200,000 years. Birds were around at the same time as the dinosaurs.

Birds are directly descended from dinosaurs: or as some scientists prefer, birds *are* dinosaurs. Modern classification, with its shift to genetics and away from morphological characteristics (that is to say, shape and form, that is to say, easily understood) means that everything in this discipline is now full of contradictions and disagreement. It's no good those of us who live away from the shopfloor taking too firm a line on anything involved in these often heated debates; we must simply deal with these matters as best we can.

Archaeopteryx, generally regarded as the first bird, dates back to the late Jurassic, 200 million years ago, right at the beginning of the age of dinosaurs. Some regard it as a dinosaur with feathers rather than a true bird: nevertheless, whatever it is, it is certainly a feath-ered creature of great antiquity. The distinction between feathered dinosaurs and actual birds has become complex and difficult in light of recent discoveries, and as we have observed before, nature isn't terribly good at hard-and-fast boundaries. However, it is clear that there were unquestionably true birds and true mammals that lived alongside true dinosaurs: mammals from about 200 million years ago, birds from 150 million.

The dinosaurs were wiped out in the great extinction of 65 million years ago, the end of the Cretaceous era, and the beginning of the Tertiary – the K-T Boundary. (This extinction was probably triggered by the earth's collision with a meteor, one of the five, or if you prefer, six great extinction episodes in the history of the earth. The sixth, according to some, is happening right now.)

With the dinosaurs gone and half the animal species on earth gone with them, and with the earth recovering from the great trauma of the impact, vast numbers of ecological niches fell vacant. Nature abhors a vacuum. There were birds and mammals who evolved to fill them: a circumstance called an adaptive radiation. And so life on earth changed dramatically once again.

Fossil evidence for small birds is hard to come by, because their delicate and hollow bones don't fossilise very easily. Most songbirds are small, adapted for feeding on insects, seeds and fruit, which makes their remains easy to overlook. The oldest passerine fossil – the group that includes all songbirds – was found in Queensland in Australia, and it is about 55 million years old. Current thinking is that the passerines evolved in Australia and New Guinea and radiated from there.

The vast passerine group divides into the suboscines and the oscines, the last being the group we call song-birds. "Songbird" is actually a loose and rather inaccurate term, and one that smacks of northern hemisphere chauvinism, but we might as well carry on using it – loosely – since this is a book mostly about northern hemisphere song. This group is distinguished from the suboscines by its greatly more complex vocal apparatus. The oscines have been a great success story, for it is best to measure evolutionary success by the number of different species produced, rather than on some imposed notion of intelligence or size or complexity or human-like characteristics. Remember that evolution isn't trying to produce some perfectly advanced and intelligent being: the job of evolution is to produce creatures capable of surviving and breeding and passing on their genes. It's not about progress; evolution has no goals beyond survival.

And in terms of species, songbirds have been phenomenally succesful, an adaptive radiation that began around 40 million years ago. The earth has been full of song for all this time. Oscines – songbirds – provide getting on for half – a good 40 per cent – of all the species of birds on earth.

Humans came to this singing and teeming world very much as an afterthought. If you wish to consider the history of the earth as a single year, then humans arrived at close to midnight on New Year's Eve. Mark Twain said, using a less up-to-date chronology: "Man has been here 32,000 years. That it took a hundred million years to prepare the world for him is proof that that is what it was done for. I suppose it is. I dunno. If the Eiffel Tower were now representing the world's age, the skin of paint on the pinnacle-knob at its summit would represent man's share of that age; and anybody would perceive that that skin was what the tower was built for. I reckon they would. I dunno."

Certainly, the most significant thing humans have achieved in those few New Year's Eve hours, or the brief coat-of-paint years, is the sixth extinction.

Greenfinch

A greenfinch sounds like a human doing really rather a good impersonation of a bird. The little whistled phrases and warbles are not precisely like those of a human whistling: rather, they sound just like a pipe made to sound like a bird; one, perhaps, that contains a little reservoir of water to create a bubbling and liquid tone. The pace is measured and relaxed, though not quite so bone idle as a blackbird's. It's pretty and varied and not immediately easy for a learning human being to pick out. That's because it sounds not so much like the music of a species but like the entire abstract concept of birdsong.

However, the greenfinch will do you a favour and every now and then insert a single utterly distinctive note, or call. It's a wheezing, buzzing glissando, whizzing easily down the scale, generally transliterated as zweeeee.

This is generally regarded as an expression of excitement, and similar sounds are used later in the season as a less extravagant piece of territorial singing. If you catch onto that zweeee, you will have your greenfinch, and from it, you will learn the pretty song that lies behind it. The greenfinch will not only sing from set places, it will also perform in flights above the territory.

How I invented music

Birds not only gave us song. They gave us instrumental music as well. Birds gave us melody. Music is life and death for birds: for humans it is the most gloriously useless thing in our lives.

Human music begins with rhythm, and rhythm is not the most obvious part of birdsong. Mammals have much stronger feelings about rhythm than birds: just about every human that was ever born entered the world after a nine-month drum solo, something that that no egg-born bird could ever know. It's only once you have been born that melody breaks in on your consciousness. And humans heard it and they sang, and then they heard it again and sought to make a sound that was closer to birds than the human voice.

The first musical instruments imitate the sound of birds. The first musical instruments were flutes. This is not, I suggest, because flutes are easy to make – it must be easier to make a twanging instrument, or melodic percussion like a xylophone. But flutes are what people first made, and they made them in order to sound like birds. Birds, they knew, are what music is.

I have sat on an open plain in Africa with a sprightly wind

blowing, looking at the bones of a long-dead warthog, with some of the bones hollowed out by hungry invertebrates. I picked up a bone and it played music, and not by my intention. I held it; the wind blew across it; it made a note. I shifted it about, so that instead of making a continuous sound, it made a series of notes. All the same note, but surely it wouldn't be hard to find a bone to make another note. And it sounded like a bird. I had invented music.

The oldest suggested date for the oldest musical instrument so far discovered is 67,000 years ago. It is called the Divje Babe flute, because it was found in the Divje Babe caves in Slovenia. It is much damaged and very fragile, and it was carved from the femur of a young cave bear, a big and impressive species that became extinct 25,000 years ago. It has a couple of holes: it is exactly what you would expect the first flute to look like. Some spoilsports dispute this, saying that it is merely a bone that has been chewed by a carnivore, one who just happened to make two very neat and symmetrical holes.

Me, I prefer the flute idea, but there are plenty more flutes, more recent but still pre-dating any other kind of instrument. There is a five-hole flute found in Ulm in Germany made from a vulture's wing bone; that's 35, 000 years old. It's natural to make a flute from a bird bone, partly because, well, it comes from a bird's body and it's supposed to make a bird's noise and perhaps that matters; and partly because bird bones are already hollow, which means that they are practically flutes already. Flutes made from swan and mammoth bones have been found near the vulture flute. Even 6,000 years ago, it was all flutes. Flutes seem to have developed in different cultures across the world. There is a collection of Chinese bone flutes 8,000 years old, and some of these have actually been played.

The earliest instruments that are not flutes are as recent as 2,600 BC, from Ur in Sumeria, where a collection of lyres and harps was found – along with plenty of flutes.

When we first started to make music beyond the limits of the human voice, we tried to sound like birds. Birds led us to music. In rhythm, we hear – we feel – our mammalian heritage. In melody, we turn to another class of vertebrates altogether. It is the fusion across the classes that has brought us music. Birds set our musical agenda: as a result we have been singing and dancing and expressing our sadness and our joy in song across the millennia.

Skylark

If the blackbird is background music, the skylark is a bird of the foreground. It's not precisely that the song is better or more complex; it's just that the song of the skylark has a way of forcing itself onto human awareness. It seems to be a bird that positively demands to be anthropomorphised: self-doomed to becoming a symbol of human aspiration and joy.

It is a bird and a song that cannot get lost. The singers we have discussed so far have mainly been birds of canopy, thicket and woodland edge: hedges, copses, gardens – places where you can't see very far in any one direction. But skylarks are birds of open spaces: the more sky, the better they like it. And when they sing, there aren't many birds around. They choose a stage – the sky – that is more or less deserted, so far as other singers are concerned, and they make it their own. Arable fields, short-grass meadows, open heath: these are the places they like to nest, and above them is where the male bird sings.

There tend to be few perches in such places, so the skylark mostly does without: singing on the wing, sometimes circling, sometimes holding still, most often climbing higher and higher, as if being hauled up to heaven on a piece of string. (See what I mean about anthropomorphising?) If you are out in a place with plenty of sky and you hear a song that continues, unbroken, without rest or even a pause for breath, this is your skylark.

Endless, unstoppable singing, with an apparently endless series of variations about this theme of perpetual music, making phrases from repeated syllables, loud, clear, and always astonishing. In vast open places you can hear many skylarks at once, each proclaiming his own few square yards of territory far below.

Never stopping. That is the heart of the skylark's song. They will frequently sing for ten minutes at a stretch: 30 minutes is not unknown. Flight is a costly business for a bird, that is why their metabolism has to be so high, why they need constant refuelling, why it is so important to protect a good source of food in order to raise young. Song is also the most colossal effort, designed to weed out the bluffers. The cost in energy of a skylark song is a thought almost as dizzying as the song itself. Does any bird put quite so much of itself into a performance?

They hold nothing back. They sing early in the day – they tend to be up with the lark – and they sing long and they sing late. They sing from on high; from the vantage point of the sky, they pour and pelt music, as Gerard Manley Hopkins wrote.

But the skylark is actually a ground bird. The feeding

and nesting and most other important parts of the bird's life are done on the floor. They are vocal birds throughout the year, and you can often hear them making rather radiophonic calls as they work the ground or fly, low, from one foodsource to another. It is only for a few brief weeks that they become birds of the sky: and they do it not so much brilliantly as miraculously.

A breath of fresh air

When does the skylark take a breath? How can he sing for so long on a single lungful of air? That seems to be the great miracle of the skylark: that so small a creature, with what must be a tiny pair of lungs, sustains himself for so long without replenishing his air supply. The greater miracle lies in the answer to those two questions: all the time, and he doesn't.

So let's play the didgeridoo. This instrument, in the hands of an accomplished player, produces a continuous sound. But when does a didgeridoo player take a breath? How can he play for so long on a single breath? All the time, and he doesn't. He uses a technique called circular breathing. It's not actually circular, though. It just seems as if it is. You take a lungful of air and fill you cheeks with the stuff. Then you use the muscles of your cheeks to squeeze air from your mouth – into your didgeridoo – while simultaneously inhaling through your nose. Once you've got the technique, you can keep going for a startling length of time. The technique is used by players of many wind instruments, both brass and woodwind. Kenny G, an American jazz virtuoso, has played a single note for 45 minutes.

Birds do real circular breathing. They do so without cheating, and that's how they operate. In a bird, the air doesn't go in and out, making a u-turn, then coming back, depleted. A bird passes air through two lungs, nine separate air sacs and even through its hollow bones. A bird's air doesn't make a u-turn and come back again, diminished of oxygen. It is not a controlled in-out with a diaphragm.

The air comes in though the nostrils, which are at the base of its bill unless it's a kiwi, which uniquely has them at the tip, or a gannet, which has no nostrils, presumably because they would be inconvenient for a bird that spends most of its life plunge-diving into the sea from a dizzy height. The air then makes a grand circle around the air cavities of the bird, which means that a bird always has fresh oxygen-rich air in its lungs, which is just perfect for a creature whose principal way of moving is the most energy-demanding method of them all: flight.

This arrangement makes it possible for birds to sing with colossal volume for their size and over apparently impossible stretches of time. What allows them to fly allows them to sing. The skylark does both at the same time: an extraordinary and vivid demonstration of all that makes a bird special.

Blithe spirit

Is there a song more beloved, more celebrated, than the skylark's? Well, maybe one, but we'll get to that at the end of the book. If you want proof that birdsong seriously matters to humans, a quick trawl through the work of the poets will provide it. And time and again they turn to skylarks. Only one other bird has provided so much joy, so many rapturous verses, so many philosophical digressions into God, the world, life and humankind. As the skylark establishes and holds his territory, so the listener below finds, himself, a new way to live and the meaning of life itself.

The skylark has inspired so many poets and so many verses because the song is truly exceptional and because nobody but a dullard could miss it. Not everybody can recognise the song itself from a mere recording, but when it comes pelting down from the sky in its endless never-pausing complexities, there is no other bird it could possibly be. I am inclined to say that the bird is so obvious that even a poet could recognise it, but that would be unworthy. John Clare was a first-rate birder, and Gerard Manley Hopkins was good enough to pick out a woodlark from the surrounding hubbub.

Clare compares the skylark with humans, and so finds a sermon on humility:

> Had they thy wing
> Like such a bird, themselves would be too proud
> And build on nothing but a passing cloud!

Shelley wrote the most famous skylark poem of all, though not the best, in my view:

> Hail to thee, blithe spirit!

The first line is part of the English language, a line everybody knows even though many have forgotten what follows:

> Bird thou never wert –
> That from heaven or near it
> Pourest thy full heart
> In profuse strains of unpremeditated art.

Again, the bird is celebrated for what it can tell us about life:

> Teach me half the gladness
> That thy brain must know;
> Such harmonious madness
> From my lips would flow,
> The world should listen, as I am listening now.

In other words, if I could write like a skylark, I'd go straight to the top of the best-seller list. Sometimes it seems that everyone who could lift a pen has had a crack at the skylark. Wordsworth had his go: "Dost thou despise the earth where cares abound?" George Meredith gave us "The Lark Ascending", though the poem doesn't live up to Vaughan Williams and the music the poem inspired in him.

Hopkins wrote two skylark poems. "The Caged Skylark" begins: "As a dare-gale skylark scanted in a dull cage… " My favourite skylark poem is Hopkins' other effort, "The Sea and the Skylark":

His rash-fresh re-winded new-skeinèd score
In crisps of curl off wild winch whirl, and pour
And pelt music, till none's to spill nor spend.

Hopkins' spontaneous joy in wild wonders is something I share, something I suspect we all share. Hopkins always brings this joy back to God, but I suspect that even with him, God is something of an afterthought. The human connection to non-human life, made possible by the sudden apprehension of wild wonders, is, for me at least, more than good enough on its own.

Modern poets have also turned to larks. Diana Hendry gives us "Skylark Researcher":

I try to pretend that they are simply out
Of fashion, like Shelley,

But secretly I am afraid
They have been hushed up ...
Or that they have worn themselves out to a frazzle
Singing their hearts out at the blank sky.

Rory McGrath was moved to lyricism in his delightful book *Bearded Tit*. It's not precisely verse, but I quote the end of the relevant chapter:

And the collective noun for skylarks?
An exaltation.
Perfect.
Peerless king of summer sky.
What a bird!
What a day. What a memory. Oh yes, I suppose I
     should say:
What a joint!

Then there is a poem by Isaac Rosenberg. It's not the best skylark poem, though pretty good, and it's certainly the most important for those interested in birdsong and what it means to humans. Rosenberg wrote it while serving at the Somme, where he was killed in 1918. He writes about the return from a night patrol into no man's land. Let's have all of it:

Sombre the night is.
And though we have our lives, we know
What sinister threat lies there.

Dragging these anguished limbs, we only know
This poison-blasted track opens on our camp –
On a little safe sleep.

But hark! joy – joy – strange joy.
Lo! heights of night ringing with unseen larks.
Music showering our upturned list'ning faces.

Death could drop from the dark
As easily as song –
But song only dropped,
Like a blind man's dreams on the sand
By dangerous tides,
Like a girl's dark hair for she dreams no ruin lies
    there,
Or her kisses where a serpent hides.

A small bird, a small birding moment gives comfort
even in hell. We would be foolish, then, surrounded as
we are by the problems, milder but no less pressing, of
the 21st century, not to seek comfort and, in the middle
of despair, find joy in the song of the birds and in the
sound of the lark ascending.

Chiffchaff

It's not a great song, not when compared to the song of the skylark, but it's one of the great moments of the year. It sounds just like one more little bird singing out of sight – but what it means is that the year has turned again: that winter, already having taken a battering from great tits and blackbirds and skylarks, is now well and truly on the run. It is the moment when the year reaches its tipping point.

And here's a thing to bring on an attack of rather agreeable smugness: not a lot of people know it. Pick out the call of the chiffchaff and you know you are a bit of a birder, and you are privy to the great secret that only birders know. You – and it seems sometimes you alone – know that when the chiffchaff chiffs and chaffs the triumph of the spring is now irreversibly upon us.

The chiffchaff is the first migrant to arrive back in Britain and start singing. It is the first because it doesn't travel so very far: southern Europe and northern Africa. It looks almost identical to the willow warbler, which, as we have seen, flies to sub-Saharan Africa, but their songs are totally different. We shall meet the willow warbler in due course, as the springtime victory becomes a rout, but let us deal now with the song of the chiffchaff.

The basic unit is in two syllables: chiff and chaff. It is quite different from the two-syllable song of the great tit, because with a chiffchaff, each syllable is equally stressed. The bird is *zilpzalp* in German, *siff-saff* in Welsh, *tjiftjaf* in Dutch. The song has some slight variations, often breaking into three syllables – chiff-chaff-chiff, chiff-chaff-chiff – and occurring in fairly distinct verses.

It tends to come from high in the canopy, and the bird itself is hard to see. So listen. When your ears are tuned in, you'll find that this first migrant tends to arrive in mid-March with something of a shout: a dramatic breaking of the patterns made by the resident birds, a promise that greater songs are yet to come – and will be arriving in the coming weeks.

Think of it. A bird travels hundreds of miles to spend the spring and summer with us, to make more birds in our country, and its song means that those who travel much greater distances, whose journeys can be measured in thousands of miles, are nearing the end of their still more incredible journeys. Each bringing its own incredible and infinitely more complex songs.

The chiffchaff is not the champion but the herald: announcing the arrival of those greater. But let us enjoy him for his own sake: as an expression of sweet doggedness, of persistence, of promise.

Some chiffchaffs are now taking advantage of our milder winters and cutting out the risks of migration altogether. This is a gamble but then migration is a gamble. The stayers bet there will be no prolonged hard and killing frost; the travellers bet that they will survive the journey, and that the refuelling stops on the migration route will still be there, undamaged. Each strategy has its winners and its losers.

But in March, the sweet and simple song comes bouncing down from the tops of the tallest trees. Time to rejoice.

Crisis relocation

If you are a nuclear strategist, you call it crisis re-location. It means being somewhere else when the disaster takes place. The birds cracked that one millions of years ago. Winter is a crisis: so it's not a bad idea to be somewhere else when it happens. So they came up with the strategy of migration.

Most – but by no means all – bird migrations are north-south. They fly away from the cold weather. Many British breeding birds spend their winters a long way from Britain: some go to southern Europe and North Africa, others go further, across the Sahara, down below the equator. One of the most moving sounds I have ever heard is the song of the willow warbler in the Kalahari. The country was arid scrub rather than true desert, but all the same, here was a sound – the sound of the cool English spring, a sweet, gentle lisping descent down the scale, but I could hear it boldly and optimistically thou-sands of miles away, in this tough, but apparently still viable place. A place deeply alien to me, it was home from home for a willow warbler that might have been my neighbour back in England.

Why bother coming back? Why not stay down in the

warmth? It's a good question. But migrant birds often go to their wintering grounds to exploit food sources that can be both considerable and erratic – fruiting trees and superabundant insect populations. These may not be enough to support a bird for 12 months of the year. And there are advantages in the northern hemisphere. Not only does the change in weather in the north bring out a seasonal bonanza of insects – adults, caterpillars and other larvae – it also brings with it very long hours of daylight. This gives a bird many more hours of foraging. That means a greater opportunity to raise a large brood, perhaps more than one brood. Britain is worth escaping from: it is also worth coming back to.

The journeys themselves are stupendous. Many of the smaller birds – the songbirds that this book celebrates more than most others – make their journeys by night. It has been suggested that this gives them an opportunity to navigate by means of the fixed stars, a more straightforward process than the calculations required to steer by the constantly-shifting sun. Most migrations follow a great circle route, the shortest distance between two points on a sphere: birds have clearly cracked spherical trigonometry.

There are other advantages to travelling by night: there is less chance of getting picked off by birds of prey, and it is easier to pick up sound signals from below, particularly the whereabouts of birds of the same species. Birds are very good birdlisteners; they have to be.

Birds of prey, and other birds that can soar – that is

to say, gain height on still wings – prefer to migrate by day, when they can exploit rising columns of air – thermals – to gain height. This is a laborious process, at least to the eye, but it is very energy-efficient. Birds of prey like ospreys, marsh harriers and hobbies migrate from this country; European storks, seldom seen in Britain, are also daytime soarers and gliders.

Birds come back to Britain because it is to their advantage to do so. It stacks up, in terms of survival, in terms of making more birds, in terms of evolution. There is no call to get sentimental about it. Nevertheless, the return of our migrant birds is a fine and emotional matter, and it is a wonderful thing to be a part of it every spring. I would say that the greatest thing of all about understanding a bit of birdsong is that it makes you hyperaware of the drama of the turning year. If you can pick out the songs of the migrants from the chorus of our resident birds, you experience a wonderful gratifying sense of the return of our faithful friends.

Of course, that last bit is horribly anthropomorphic; I know that. The birds are here for themselves, not for us. But we are certainly entitled to enjoy their return: to celebrate the fabulous achievement of the epic double journey, to greet familiar birds on their return, to know that with every migrant that arrives our own weather gets better, warmer and easier. One swallow doesn't make a summer, but the first one tells us pretty unambiguously that more swallows are on their way: that spring is here and that summer will follow.

This is something that touches us on a very deep level. Before we had houses and central heating, the winter was for us humans, as it was for the birds, very much a thing to struggle through and survive. Crisis relocation was not an option for humans. The birds could be envied and admired for their winter absence – even if no one was precisely sure where they went to, or if they stayed around but hibernated – and celebrated when they returned to our lives. We can celebrate what it means to the birds, and what it means to us: the turning of the year, the beginning of better times.

The few weeks from mid-April to mid-May bring us a chorus in which one new singer follows the next. You've heard the blackcap, can the willow warbler be far behind? One singer, then another, then another: till by May the country echoes with song.

Cuckoo

The cuckoo's is perhaps the ultimate birdsound. It might have been created so that humans can mimic it. It might have been created so that even the dullest and least musical human could recognise it. It might have been created so that humans have a cue to celebrate the spring and the summer that follows.

Sumer is icumen in!
Lhude sing cucu!

The song – summer is a-coming in, loudly sing cuckoo – is a round, and is reckoned by some to be the oldest piece of counterpoint of this type in existence. It dates back to the 13th century and includes the immortal line "bucke verteth", or "the stag farts": as he is perfectly entitled to do when full of spring grass.

The sound of the cuckoo is the sound of celebration. Cuckoos turn up in song and other pieces of music time and again. We find them irresistible. You can hear them in Vivaldi's *Four Seasons*, and in Beethoven's Sixth, two of the world's most beloved bits of music. The two-note call is loud and it carries for miles.

That is rather the point. Cuckoos don't hold a territory in the normal way. They don't need to hold onto a place with the resources to feed a brood of little cuckoos. They delegate that part of their lives, giving rise to a vast set of stories and myths and metaphors and moralisings across the ages. The cuckoo of the British countryside is not unique in this practice of nest-parasitism, though it's the only British bird that goes in for it. There are many other nest-parasitising species of cuckoo across the world, for a start. There are also other groups that parasitise: the various species of indigo bird of Africa each parasitise a different species. Outside the breeding season they are very drab and more or less indistinguishable, but you can tell them apart, if you are very good indeed, because they mimic the song and call of their unwitting hosts.

Even if you don't have a territory, you still need to get in touch with a cuckoo of the opposite sex if you want to fulfil your biological destiny. You need a partner before the process of egg-laying in a stranger's nest can begin. But having no need of a territory, these birds scatter over wide distances. The call needs to be big, then. It also needs to be simple and far carrying: too complex a song would get lost and confused. I have heard the many different species of cuckoo in Africa giving loud, bold, simple and equally memorable calls for the same reason. In Africa, the cuckoos' calls are associated with the coming of the rains, while the cuckoo we know is associated with the coming of the warm weather. But it's all the same equation: water plus sun equals life. It's just that we are always waiting for the sun, and in Africa they are always waiting for the rain. In parts of Africa, they rejoice at the sound of the red-chested cuckoo, because they know the rains cannot be much longer delayed. We rejoice at the sound of our own cuckoo because he brings us the sun. Both cuckoos bring life.

The sound of all the cuckoos is intended to ring out over vast distances, a male imploring a female to seek him out. It's sometimes referred to as a stud-post call. Cuckoos are mostly solitary, but their need for others of their kind is expressed in the far-reaching call. No cuckoo is an island.

Cuckoos – our cuckoos – also make a loud, bubbling cry, which is always surprising, always making even an experienced birdlistener start and wonder, if only for a second, what the hell is going on.

But that simple double-note – occasionally stretched into a triple-note by a truly excited bird – is part of our heritage. It has been the subject of a thousand letters to *The Times*: the cuckoo is a bird that bursts the barriers of mere birding and becomes a concern of the entire populace. The cuckoo gives us the birdsong for everybody. It is a bird of one season, but the best of seasons.

Last cuckoo?

But when did you last actually hear a cuckoo? There have been years when I have failed to hear one at all: something that just a few years ago would have been unthinkable for anyone but the most determined urbanite. Cuckoos were everywhere, or at least their sound was: in suburbia, across the countryside, wherever there were open spaces and trees.

Cuckoos have undergone a drastic decline in the last 30 years. And here's a still sadder thing: other long-distance migrants are also getting scarcer. It seems that a way of life that has worked brilliantly for millions of years is now threatened.

I have found willow warblers hard to come by, outside optimal habitat. They used to be everywhere. House martins are much scarcer: there used to be a dozen nests around my house every spring; now there are none. The way of the long-distance migrant is getting harder with every passing year.

And it is hard to know what to do. That's because a journey so long covers so much land. How can you protect every yard of so long a journey? The journey is made tougher as the Sahara Desert gets wider. This is happening for a complex interrelated suite of reasons. Birds need feeding stops on the way – refuelling stations, as it were. Sometimes these are protected, but many have been damaged, making the journey – one that always exists not far from the edge of the possible – still tougher. The wintering grounds are changing all the time under the pressure of increasing human populations. And many of the breeding grounds – the British bit –have been damaged and destroyed, and this is a process that continues. All birds, all wildlife, are up against it: but the long-distance migrants now have the toughest job of all.

It is not my purpose to make this a book of doom and gloom. I want to celebrate birds and their music, and all that it means to us lucky humans who can tune in and enjoy the concert. But I must level with you here and say that the long-term future for migrating birds is an intractable problem, and one that is becoming critical.

We are in the process of losing the birds that bring us the greatest joy.

Swallow

Migration was one of the great discoveries of the natural world. Even deep in the 19th century, the fact that birds were world travellers was not widely known or accepted. It was one of those mysteries: swallows appeared in the spring and disappeared in the winter, but nobody knew what happened in between. The popular theory was that they spent their winters hibernating at the bottom of ponds. As usual, the truth turned out to be a lot weirder than the stuff we made up.

Swallows are archetypal migrants: everybody's idea of what a migrant bird should be. That's because they are so very noticeable. They catch the eye, not because they are terribly bright in colour, but because they are always on the move, and spectacular movers at that. Their flight silhouette is very distinct: swept back wings and long tail: a bit like a fighter jet. That's not exactly coincidence: like a fighter jet they are fast and very manoeuvrable, constantly shifting out of straight and level flight to collect insects on the wing.

They arrive and, in the nicest possible way, they seem to take over the place. Suddenly they are everywhere.

That's because they have a great affinity for most human spaces outside cities. They like open meadows, preferably full of grazing livestock, cricket fields, watercourses: and always, they draw the eye with their agility. They are birds to cheer you up: jaunty and indomitable and apparently approving of humankind.

They draw the ear, too. They are very gabby birds. The first swallow of summer is a good moment for most of us: if your ears are tuned in, this moment will often come earlier, because you will be alerted by the song. They like to sing in snatches on the wing, a brisk and rather wheezy twittering, a merry and excited jumble of notes. They will give a more prolonged and considered version of the song from a perch.

Swallows have adapted to human habitations very well, and love to make nests in outbuildings: under carports, in garages (don't close the door on them) and in barns and stables: Americans call the same species barn swallow. They nest in my stables, and carry on the business of feeding their young as I muck out beneath them, flying in at the door always with the same cheerful double-note of warning. As the summer progresses, the young swallows leave the nest and perch along the joists in a row, formal as a class of schoolchildren, leaving a neatly ruled line of whitewash on the concrete beneath. They wheeze and chatter to each other, and gape excitedly as the parent birds fly in with refreshments. Soon they have learned to fly, and they swing and curvet around the outbuildings, making amateurish attempts to catch insects. Then the parents set to work on a second brood: the advantages of the long, long summer days are obvious.

As the days shorten, the birds will line up along the telegraph wires, chattering away to each other, preparing for the long journey back. How many miles do they cover? For often they fly not in a direct line but in a series of swooping, feeding circles. A day arrives when you notice that you haven't seen or heard a swallow for a few days. Then you have to wait for them to return: that swift chattering on the wing, and the one swallow that doesn't – or maybe does – make a summer.

Vertebrate chauvinism

Birdsong is not just the song of birds. It is the sound of life. That's not a fluffy generalisation: it is a plain fact. In spring, life rekindles, and the more of it there is in any one place, the more birdsong you will hear if you go there. Tune into birdsong and you are tuning into life itself: because if there weren't a great many other forms of life, there would be no birdsong. Birdsong is, if you like, the tip of the iceberg of life: each singing bird is perched on a songpost constructed from a great mountain of other forms of life, some of it mysterious and most of it largely unnoticed by us humans. The song of birds tells us that it is all there, that it is all happening, that it is all still working.

The basis of all life is the sun, the ultimate source of energy for all life on earth – barring, of course, those strange creatures that live off hydrothermal vents, but we need not trouble with those right now, since there are very few singing birds at the bottom of the ocean. The sun fires the vegetation: the great rekindling of the spring takes place with new leaves, flowers, growth. These provide food for many animals. We are too used to thinking only in terms of backboned animals, and our vertebrate chauvinism blinds us to the richness of life beyond our own kind. There are, for example, 2,000 species of moth that can be found in this country. There are 242 species of wasp recorded in Surrey alone.

There are insects in uncountable numbers, in terms of both individuals and species. A walk beneath the trees will repeatedly take you through clouds of midges, hanging in the air, dancing, waiting to compete for females. A flowering bush will be ferociously buzzing. Early spring will bring the fast and mobile male orange-tip butterfly, purposefully seeking a mate: as notice-able as a bird, if less noisy. Every wood is crawling with caterpillars which most of us will never notice, while the great caterpillar-noticers, like blue tits and great tits, call above us to tell us all about them. If they didn't kill hundreds of caterpillars every day, they would not be up there and singing.

There are invertebrates everywhere. They can be found on leaves and branches and twigs, underground, in rotting vegetation, in piles of shit, in the water, over the water, in the air close to the ground, in the air high above. Tiny spiderlings will creep to the top of a stem of grass and let out a long thread of silk, to catch the wind and go ballooning, a recognised form of spider transit. Some eventually find the ground and a way of life, others get eaten from the air.

Spring is a great bonanza. Not just for birds, but for everything that lives, everything that seeks to make profit from the golden time of year, to grow, to make offspring, to fulfil genetic and evolutionary destinies, to make life carry on.

This whole vast unfathomable process is summed up for us humans not in the counting of midges and the sampling of spiderlings, but in the song of birds. Without the millions of insects in the air that get in our eyes and plague us, without the spiders to scare us, without the bugs that bug us, there are no swallows to make a summer. Each note of birdsong is a miracle: one that has cost many lives.

Pigeons

It is easy to treat pigeons and doves as if they were all the same: one great flock of flying rats and pestiferous crop-destroyers, cooing indiscriminately from somewhere above our heads. The fact is that there are five species of pigeon and dove in Britain, and if you want to listen to the best and most thrilling of them, you need to separate him from all the rest.

Feral pigeon

Let's start with feral pigeons. And also with racing pigeons, city pigeons, fancy white doves in the dovecote, fantails, tumblers, pouters and rollers. They are all descended from the rock dove, which can still be found in a more or less pure state in isolated and rocky parts of this country. But rock doves have been domesticated for centuries, and they have been selectively bred for all sorts of different reasons. Humans began to keep and breed rock doves because it was pretty easy and they are pretty edible, a double win for humans, and arguably for the birds themselves. Even after they were no longer bred as convenient protein, people kept them because they liked having them around. They were bred for all kinds of mad reasons: there are literally hundreds of breeds of pigeon. It's the same with dogs, and as with dogs, every breed is ultimately a member of the same species. Charles Darwin was fascinated by pigeons. He used to keep them, and he loved to hang out with the top pigeon-fanciers, the masters of fancy breeding. It was all part of his great work *The Origin of Species*. Darwin reasoned that if humans can change an animal dramatically over relatively few generations by means of selective breeding – artificial selection, he called it – then over the long term, with nature rather than humans in charge, and natural rather than artificial selection as the principle behind it all, even more dramatic changes might be made.

So it is important to pick your feral pigeon from the rest: and it's a good throaty, rather purring coo.

Wood pigeon

The other four pigeons we will touch on here are all good species, quite separate from rock doves and feral pigeons. The wood pigeon is an uncompromised wild bird, though it does well in towns so long as there are gardens, parks and mature trees. The call is more complex and rhythmic than the rock dove/feral pigeon's. The best mnemonic is the advice the bird gives to the cattle-rustling Welshman: steal *twoooo* cows, Taffy. Others, perhaps Welshmen, may prefer: my toe *is* bleeding. Wood pigeons are also great clappers: they like to cruise over their territory and rise to clap their wings together, a surprisingly loud sound, designed to tell any other wood pigeons that this clapping bird happens to be in very fine shape. You can quite often tell a wood pigeon from the way it gets startled: no bird explodes from a tree in quite so dramatic a fashion, with a wild scattering of twigs. You can hear this sound as you pass beneath the tree, often if you do so at dusk and the bird has settled for the night, making the walker feel both guilty at disturbing it and resentful at the bird's lack of trust.

Collared dove

Over the last half-century, the collared dove has made itself at home in suburbs and villages, relishing the places where humans live in a slightly less constricted way. They spread quite naturally and spontaneously: neat, pretty birds that look ever so slightly like angels when they take off, and which sound ever so slightly like dismal football fans when they sing. It's a pretty monotonous sort of a din: U-*nigh*-ted, U-*nigh*-ted, U-*nigh*-ted. The Greeks have a prettier explanation, which might improve the song for you. The bird's scientific name is *Streptopelia decaocto*, or the eighteener dove. The story is that Jesus was on his way to his crucifixion and horribly thirsty. He saw an old woman selling milk and asked her for a glass. She said it cost 18 drachmas. Jesus said he only had 17. Eighteen, she insisted. Eighteen. *Dekka-okto, dekka-octo.* So she was turned into a dove, and her meanness is commemorated every time she opens her beak: *dekka-okto dekka-okto.* Collared doves are prone to outbreaks of song at any time of the year, though naturally, they do a lot more of it in the spring.

Stock dove

One more dove before I get to the migrant, and this might win the prize for the most overlooked bird in the country, since it is such a very pigeony sort of pigeon. It's the size of a wood pigeon, but without the flashy white bits. It has very few distinguishing features. The song is equally overlookable (overlistenable?) but it is worth picking out. It is basically a series of repeated coos, so strongly expressed that there is almost a second syllable in every coo. The song builds up in a series of intensely repeated coos. It is, somehow, an unambiguously sexual song. They are great nesters in hollow trees, and they also love to get inside barn-owl boxes, and have colonised the one at my place for some years. I have to tell myself that they are, if I but knew it, more important than barn owls, being amber-listed worldwide. Not as dramatic as a barn owl – few birds are – but their song is one to pick out and congratulate yourself on, and ultimately, one to cherish.

Which brings us to the voice of the turtle.

Turtle dove

For lo, the winter is past, the rain is over and gone; the flowers appear on the earth; the time of the singing of birds is come, and the voice of the turtle is heard in our land. Lovely lines – has the coming of spring ever been better summarised? – from "The Song of Solomon", that gloriously racy book of the Bible that has sustained many a worshipper though a long sermon.

Not a turtle that swims in the sea. A turtle dove. Nothing to do with turtle turtles: it is called a turtle dove because it goes turr-turr. Its scientific name is *Streptopelia turtur*. It purrs, languid and sleepy, from the tops of trees in the late spring. It's a bird that makes the sound of cricket matches, chestnut trees bearing candles, beer in the garden and dozing in a deckchair: a sound of spring as an achievement and summer itself as more than a promise: a sound full of a thousand things all English and good and rather dated.

Alas, the song of the turtle is heard less often in our land these days, not least because the Maltese insist on shooting migrating turtle doves as they fly over their Godforsaken island. As if migrants didn't have it hard enough. For that reason, they are a special treat to hear: purring softly and rather thoughtfully, a sound that seems to encapsulate the notion of contentment: a lost world in which there was always honey still for tea. This is a sound to rejoice in, and the bird – perhaps even more than most migrants – is a bird to cherish.

Why warblers

Perhaps the whole point of learning birdsong is warblers. Warblers are a bit like chapter three of *Ulysses*. You read the first two chapters, which go off with great pace and bounce, and you can't see why anyone ever claimed the book was at all difficult. And then you get a chapter that begins: "Ineluctable modality of the visible: at least that if no more: thought through my eyes. Signatures of all things I am here to read…"

This is the point at which the more timid readers give up – and it is when you turn to the pages of the warblers in your field guide that many a would-be birder does the same thing. You look at this page, or pages, full of very small birds. They are all browny-olivey-greeny-greyish, and you think that you will never be able to tell one from another because they all look the same. So why even start? Stick with robins and blue tits: be comfortable with that.

So let me tell you something. I am not very good at telling one warbler from another myself. Not by looking at them. Very few people are. With some warblers, it is almost impossible to tell species apart by details of plumage. Put a dead bird in the hands of a museum worker, and he will puzzle about beak length and leg colour and length of the longest primary feather, and will come back to you eventually with the conclusions that it is probably a willow warbler, though it might actually be a chiffchaff.

But I can tell them apart in about half a second without needing to look at them. That's because their songs are very different. And that's how warblers work. They maintain their integrity as a species not by looking different but by sounding different. Roughly the same colouring and body shape suits several different species, but they don't get confused because it is quite impossible to muddle their songs.

The warblers are the ultimate group of birds for the birdlistener. Listening is the only practical way to tell them apart. They tend to be very hard to see at the best of times, singing from cover, feeding and living their lives away from casual eyes. You don't want to look for them: I very seldom try. I listen for them: and that is the point. It is not the bird but the song that is brightly coloured.

There are about 350 species of Old World warblers. The New World warblers need not trouble us here: they a completely different group, and one to the address of New World birders, and also of British twitchers, who get so excited when these little birds turn up over here as sad lost windblown strays. Old World warblers are all pretty small; most of them eat insects and spiders and little else. They tend to be drab in appearance. They also turn up in Africa and Asia, often as resident birds; there are eight species in Australia.

We are concerned here with the British lot. There are two resident species. The Dartford warbler is rather an advanced bird for now: they are birds that you have to go looking for on certain lowland heaths in southern England. Cetti's warblers live, and can be found in increasing numbers, around wetlands. The other warblers are all commuters, some going to southern Europe and northern Africa, others going down below the Sahara. (Some of the short-haul migrants, like chiffchaff and blackcap, as we have seen, over-winter in this country in small numbers.) There are a dozen or so that routinely concern the British birder: in this book we will deal only with the basic warblers. Look on this book, if you like, as a phrasebook, something that will let you ask the way to the station and order a Pernod without giving you enough French to read Proust ... but hoping, all the same, to set you off on the path that leads there.

Not that the basic warblers lack profundity. The acquisition of basic warbler vocabulary is a wonderfully significant journey. It is in this sudden understanding of the unseen world that you realise how much life there is all around, and how diverse it is.

Warblers really are the key to it all: the key to bird-song, and if you will, the key to life. Warblers tend to sing more when they breed in the temperate parts of the world, generally because the birds are closely

packed together. A reasonably dense population stimu-
lates singing: territorial issues become critical and that
means song. I remember a year when there was a much
higher density of sedge warblers than usual. I had never
rated the sedge warbler as a singer, but when I visited
Minsmere, the RSPB reserve in Suffolk, the place was
echoing with sedge warblers: more beautiful and far
more varied than I had ever heard before. I was deeply
impressed – even though it wasn't me they were trying to
impress. It was each other. Only the finest singers were
going to breed that year, and that simple fact brought
the best from them. That's how warblers operate. They
live by means of song. Don't bother looking for them:
open your ears instead.

Blackcap

A lot of warblers don't actually warble. We've already met the chiffchaff, which is a warbler all right, even though its common name doesn't include the word warbler. It looks almost identical to its close relative, the willow warbler – but doesn't actually warble, not in the sense of giving out a bubbling, tuneful and rather rapid series of notes. The blackcap is also a warbler. It is not called a warbler – but when it comes to warbling notes, it's probably the champion. I hope I have made myself perfectly obscure here. (The point to cling to, if you are at all confused, is biodiversity. There are lots of different sorts of warbler: by beginning to understand a few of them, you are beginning to understand the still greater mystery of biodiversity.)

The blackcap is many people's favourite songbird; some declare that it out-sings the nightingale. John Clare wrote a blackcap poem and called it the March Nightingale: a bird that arrives and sings earlier than the nightingale, which doesn't get going till late April. The blackcap has also been called the northern nightingale, because its range in this country is much greater than that of the nightingale: they've been heard, in these days of changing climate, as far north as the Orkneys.

It's a wonderfully fruity and fluty song at its peak: a song with a real richness about it. It seems that the bird is relishing each note. Even when the song is rapid, it seems to make a special effort to make each note exactly right. It's perhaps the most melodic garden singer apart from the blackbird, which is much slower and laid-back, and less rich and intense in individual notes.

The blackcap tends to sings in verses: generally beginning with some harsh and scratchy notes, which shift effortlessly into the heart of the song, these hyper-rich fluting notes, and then ending each verse with something of a flourish.

These birds mostly winter around the Mediterranean, though increasing numbers now stay over for the winter; also, a good few birds that breed in Germany and Austria winter in Britain. The Mediterranean base puts blackcaps among the short-haul migrants, which means they are likely to make an early start into the British spring, though not as early as the chiffchaffs. Listen out for them at the beginning of April, and when you find a bird that breaks the pattern of those you have already learned, look up blackcap and see if it fits.

Their contact and alarm calls are pretty distinctive, usually described as like two stones being knocked together. You'll find them anywhere there is a decent amount of vegetation: they are not as fussy as some warblers and don't insist on a closed canopy or continuous cover. They are as adaptable as they are tuneful, and that has made them something of a success story. There are generally two breeding blackcaps at my place every year, and each one uses its same favourite tree – both of them hawthorns – as its principal songpost. Puts a spring in my step every time I walk past.

Demise of the willow wren

Up until the 18th century, there was a British bird known as the willow wren. Then one of the greatest birders – one of the greatest naturalists; one of the greatest scientists in history – realised that the willow wren was actually three distinct species. Gilbert White worked out, by means of brilliant field observation, unaided by 21st-century binoculars, by state-of-the-art recording equipment, by podcasts, by field guides, by birding apps on his iPhone, by friendly local experts, that the willow wren is actually the chiffchaff, the willow warbler and the wood warbler. He was able to do this because he took the revolutionary step of observing living creatures rather than killing them and then describing the dead skin. And more than anything else he listened. He was perhaps the greatest birdlistener of all time: and it was by listening that he found three birds where there had once been one. Three songs: that could only mean three distinct species. The way we understand the wild world was changed gently, subtly, permanently.

He was the original parson-naturalist. He was curate of the parish of Selborne in Hampshire on four separate occasions. He confined his studies to one little chunk of countryside: and by doing so he changed the way human beings understand the wild world. His letters, to Thomas Pennant, a British zoologist, and to Daines Barrington, a Fellow of the Royal Society, were put together and published in 1789 as *The Natural History and Antiquities of Selborne* and they have never been out of print. His achievement was as revolutionary as anything else that was happening in the year of publication.

He studied Selborne as a whole, as a living, constantly changing entity, what we would now call an ecosystem, and as such, he invented ecology. He studied the behaviour of the animals he watched, and so invented ethology. He was particularly caught up in the signs of the changing seasons, and recorded, over 25 years, the emergence and reappearances of 400 species of plants and animals, and as such, he invented phenology. He was the first scientist to describe the harvest mouse and the noctule bat. He was, in his understated and deeply modest way, a genius.

He was a genius of the commonplace, a master of the ordinary. He saw the stuff of daily life in the country and by his power of observation, he was able to imbue everything with meaning, not just for himself but for everybody. Every line he wrote is full of love and respect: he loved the wild world, but also, in a curiously modern sense, he believed that it mattered and that it had a right to exist. He was also a pioneer in seeing the wild world as a place of pleasure and solace and adventure and excitement. He was a scientist: he was also an enthusiast. He invented birding: that is to say, watching birds as something a wise person does for pleasure. He invented the notion of taking a country walk and looking at stuff and knowing about stuff and learning about stuff as a natural and sensible way to behave.

Perhaps his greatest talent was curiosity. When he wondered what something was, he had to find out. When he wondered why, he would worry away at the question for years. He never ceased to wonder about swallows. Did they fly away somewhere? Or did they hibernate at the bottom of ponds? He never got to the bottom of that one – but he kept asking, he kept wondering, and in that alone, he is an example to us all, scientists or not.

I hope you are now beginning to solve the warbler conundrum, that you have already begun to pick out individual singers from the background music of bird-song. And as you do so, I hope very much that you are also beginning to achieve a deeper relationship with the wild world. Now you can, I hope, hear blackcaps where you once heard nothing but a cheery din. You are increasingly aware that chiffchaffs and willow warblers and wood warblers are different from each other. So it is pleasant every now and then to doff a cap to Gilbert White. The parson who changed the way we see the world.

So now we'd better learn why the willow warbler is

not a chiffchaff or, for that matter, a wood warbler, or
for that matter, a willow wren.

Willow warbler

It was when I first separated willow warbler from the rest that I knew I was forever committed as a bird-listener. It was a matter that brought me a deep and still-lasting happiness. Perhaps I shouldn't try and build the willow warbler up too much, because it's not really the greatest of songs. On the other hand – well, I think in some ways it *is* the greatest of songs. It has a special significance for me, anyway. It's my song, if you like.

A year or so back, I acquired a canoe. Not the sort of thing you do the Eskimo roll in, at least, not on purpose. It's a Canadian, and it has a special place for your beer can and a locker for your sandwiches. I keep it on the banks of the River Waveney, the boundary between Suffolk and Norfolk, and my default outing is a little paddle upstream and back again, in a section of the river that is very little built-around, and not over-controlled. The banks are busy with vegetation. And in April and early May, this section is more or less wall-to-wall willow warblers, and that makes it a sustained paddle of joy. There are five or six other warbler species, all of which – this being a pretty silent mode of travel – I am able to listen to as I pass by. But the willow warblers set the tone.

I first got the song fixed in my head when writing a book about a year in the life of Minsmere, the great RSPB reserve in Suffolk. I was doing a bird survey with the then assistant warden Rob Macklin, now the head of the eastern region of the RSPB. And as we walked, we picked up willow warblers, by their song, naturally, and each time we heard one, Rob recorded the exact spot on a map. And there were so many that by the time the day was over, I knew I would never again hear a willow warbler without knowing what it was.

And every year it comes to me as a shattering trumpet blast: an ear-splitting klaxon that screams the achievement of spring. That's despite the fact that it is the softest and gentlest of songs: a sweet lisping descent down the scale, almost an arpeggio. Each verse is about three seconds long; each rises briefly to a peak and then fades to a conclusion. It is a gentle little piece: though it's life and death to the deeply territorial willow warblers. There is a fair amount of subtle variation involved, which makes it a bird you can sit and listen to. Or paddle past with immense slowness.

They will sing their verse, pause, sing again from the same spot: gently persistent, gently insistent that this piece of Britain is theirs. They have become scarcer in some places in recent years, so they no longer seem to be a bird you have by right. They have become more of a treat, more of a special bird. That's why it always feels especially good when you find yourself in the bird's optimum habitat: the sort of place where this particular species does best. Like, for example, the riverine thickets of England; like, rather more surprisingly, the north of Scotland. It is getting ever harder to be a long-distance migrant, but it seems that the willow warblers who make an extra effort and travel still further north get a reward for their pains.

Willow warblers are territorial birds wherever they are, and they will often sing strongly later in the year when they are working on a second brood. They will also sing out on their wintering grounds in Africa. They are amazing little birds: so small, such courageous travellers, so sweet a voice, such fierce competitors. It is when you can hear the first willow warbler of the spring and know it for what it is that you have passed the point of no return. You have finished and revelled in chapter three of *Ulysses*. You have become a birdlistener. You are committed. And once you have done that, you know that a lifetime of pleasure lies before you. Once you have cracked the willow warbler, you're a goner.

First Year Birdlistening

Turn on, tune in

You can now, I hope, recognise a good few birds without seeing them. That is to say, you can hear their voices and know their names. That is a beginning, and a great one. It is a beginning, not just because there are many more songs and calls to learn, but also because birdlistening is about a great deal more than identification. If it were just a process of knowing that teacher-teacher equals great tit and down-the-scale lisping equals willow warbler, the whole thing would not be much more than a clever trick.

If you switch on the radio and hear a piece that is unmistakably Bach, you don't then switch off because your job is done. ID is just the start of the process. Let's go back to the willow warbler. The song, once logged in your brain, is unmistakable. But when you hear a willow warbler and make the correct identification, you haven't exhausted the possibilities. People used to talk about bird-spotting: spot a bird, make the ID, move on. Birdwatching is actually about watching birds: using birds as a way of understanding the world. Birdlistening is part of the same process. You identify your bird with your ears: but it need not stop there. You can listen.

You can pick out subtle variations, certain indications that this bird is singing as an individual, not just as a member of a species. You may not wish to analyse this technically, but it is something that you can't help but be aware of as you tune in.

The urgency and intensity of individuals also vary. They also vary according to the time of year, the type of habitat and the number of rival singers. Every sound-scape reflects the nature of the habitat, the season of the year and the time of the day. Sense of place and time is, in some ways, what birding, what looking at the wild world, is all about. A half-decent birdlistener can be transported across space and time blindfolded, land anywhere in Britain in any season and have a decent guess at when and where he is. A genius could do this all over the world. Even I could do it in the Luangwa Valley in Zambia.

By becoming a birdlistener, you are increasing your understanding of the world and the way it works. Birds are associated with place: you don't get a duck in a desert or a willow warbler in Piccadilly Circus. They are also associated with time: it would be truly disturbing to see a swallow in Britain in January or to hear a skylark singing on Christmas day. By listening to birds, you are acquiring an understanding of the rhythm of the planet: not in a dry factual way, but with the deep intuitive certainties of our ancestors.

And as you listen, you become, in the same deep way, aware of the importance of the many. The more you listen, the more birds there are around, and the more species of bird. You become aware that you are just one part of a living landscape: and that this landscape has many more participants than you had been aware of. You can, I hope, now walk through a wood in the spring and pick out maybe a dozen species. You are, then, aware at a very deep level that the world is not a monoculture. Nor is it a biculture: a far more usual human error. The world does not comprise humans on the one hand and everything else on the other. Humans are participants in a system of millions: and by hearing birds you are constantly reminded of the fact that the world is no biculture.

It is my hope that you, dear reader, have reached the end of your first spring as a birdlistener. You will then be aware of a number of different species of bird, and as a result, aware of a great number of deeper and far more important things. Still greater things will come in your second spring. But birds make sounds throughout the year, so as we take the pause between spring and spring, we will pick out some of the other sounds that birds make.

Seagulls

The trouble with tuning into birdsong is that it's hard to untune. And that can be frustrating. The birds covered in the first chunk of this book have mostly been birds you come across in gardens, parks, commons, suburbs, and birds of the accessible dog-walking countryside. But if you go to other places, other birds will make other noises – and you will hear them and wonder what they are.

Sometimes, this is like starting all over again. The point to hold onto is that this process is not without its pleasures. On my friend's farm in Australia, or when making a trip to any part of the Americas, I find myself struggling, but once I've got a few calls logged in the brain, I begin to see a pattern instead of anarchy. Elsewhere in the world I have done a bit more birding, and have at least somewhere to start – but then all at once I am baffled again: a bird I have forgotten, a bird I half remember, a bird I have never encountered before: and they all sound the same …

So let's go to the seaside. Spring is over: summer holiday has begun. And you arrive and hear seagulls. There are half a dozen species of gull you might readily encounter in this country: is it possible to separate all the screams and yelps and wahs and make sense of them?

Gulls don't sing. They are not territorial in the manner of songbirds. But they are a gabby lot: it's just that their range of vocabulary is used for slightly different reasons. A lot of the more spectacular and memorable calls are used in display. That is to say, it is part of a demonstration of a bird's strength: a demonstration of potential aggression without actually fighting. The birds can almost always see each other – not always the case with songbirds when they are singing – and so the voice is there to back up intimidatory flight or posture. With a songbird, sound is the primary method of communication; with a bird in display, the sound is secondary. This sound is seldom complex: it is not intended to be. It is dramatic, though: and that's precisely the point. The bird is, after all, showing off.

Herring gull

The archetypal seagull call – the noise that we think of whenever we hear the world "seagull" – is a display call of the herring gull: that series of repeated screams you hear at the start of *Desert Island Discs*, the sound that says at once, in any film, any television costume drama, that we are now at the seaside. Gulls have a decent repertoire of calls, but they are all expressed with the same kind of voice. You can often recognise other herring-gull calls because the display call is so much a part of us, and other calls are recognisably the same bird: monosyllabic squeals and yelps, and a muttered comment, generally in three syllables.

Black-headed gull

The black-headed gull is the most common British gull, but it is less inexorably associated with seaside and harbour than the others. This is the most inland of the gulls, the one you find at landfill sites and rubbish tips: a splendid white swarm in the air, as if a dump were the most thrilling place on earth; the air filled with harsh screams, screams that generally slide down the scale at the end, a sound as soothing as fingernails scraping down a blackboard. It's not much of a call on its own, but when you hear thousands of cries all at once, it really is rather splendid. Every time you encounter any species of bird in big numbers, it feels like a blow for the wild world against the oppressors – so here is a screaming air force of defiant white-winged freedom-fighters. This basic scream can be varied in intensity so that it is suitable for all sorts of different occasions. In threat display, the scream is constantly repeated.

When you move onto the other regularly encountered gulls, the lesser and the great black-backed gulls, you find yourself getting a little speculative as you listen to their calls. The lesser has a slightly different twang from a herring gull's: more nasal, more reedy, some suggest. The great is gruffer and deeper, as befits a much bigger bird. I haven't included these birds on the podcast, because I am trying to avoid confusing you at this delicate stage of your education. But here is a good exercise: sit outside a seaside pub or some pleasant spot along the prom and watch the gulls as they call. You might as well take advantage of the fact that they are doing it in plain view. Time for a drink: I'm trying to separate herring gull from lesser black-backed.

Kittiwake

One more gull, one you will encounter if you visit wilder and rockier parts of the country in late spring and early summer. The cry of the kittiwake is much wilder, much less circumscribed than the voices of the other gulls. This is not an inland bird at all: this bird would turn its beak up at the mere suggestion of a landfill site. These are birds of the open ocean – pelagic birds – but they come in to nest on cliffs and never do so without making an immense din. The main call is a wild and moaning two-syllable scream, but the bird will also, quite pedantically, enunciate the three syllables of its own name with a firm stress on the last. For the birdlistener, this plaintive scream is a sound that takes your mind to those places where you can't see land in any direction at all: an alarming thought for most humans but sweet home for the kittiwake.

Swift

I have developed a rather fine ritual. Once a year, in early summer, I go to the local pub in Suffolk with my older boy. We sit on a bench placed unpromisingly by the car park. I have never seen anyone else sit on it. It looks straight down the short country street, which has a couple of dozen houses on one side of it, houses that have been there a while. And we sit there and enjoy our drinks and settle back to enjoy the cabaret.

And here they come, screaming at the tops of their voices, rooftop level, two dozen of them at once, all going like the clappers. Swifts: and what is not inaptly known as a screaming party.

Swifts have probably edged out the swallow as Britain's favourite migrant, largely because the swift is more comfortable in cities than the swallow. If they can find nesting places – the roof-spaces of old buildings being their favourite – and a sky full of insects, they have all they need. They are fliers, the most aerial of all birds, and perhaps the most spectacular. Not in colour: blackish-grey and greyish-black just about covers it. But their speed is colossal, and they love to fly about together. And when they do, they often scream.

It can't be compared in beauty to the tinkling of the swallow, or any of the songs from the warblers. But for sheer extravagant drama, the combination of the flashing bird and the reckless scream is a hard thing to beat. They are among the last birds to arrive in this country for the spring and the first to leave; they go almost before summer has started. They are with us for a scant three months. When they arrive, they form screaming parties to sort out such vital questions as who mates with whom. When that point has been established, the adolescent, non-breeding birds often form screaming parties for the sheer hell of it. And as the brief season comes to an end, all the swifts will start to form screaming parties as they get themselves psyched up for the long journey back to Africa.

Swifts are pretty swift fliers in normal life, when they can cruise at 26 mph or 43 kph, their default speed as they move from place to place or hawk for insects across the sky. But in screaming parties they get competitive, and go for sheer blinding speed, radically altering their aerodynamics and their wing profile as they do so. In such a state, swifts have been reliably measured at 69.3 mph, 111.6 kph. This makes them the fastest bird recorded in straight and level flight; and they can even hold this speed when flying upwards. Peregrine falcons are faster, but only in the stoop when they employ the force of gravity to add to their speed. Swifts reach – and sustain – their speed unaided.

Screaming as they go: a wild and glorious sound, a

sound that makes you want to hurl a few necessities into a bag and fly with them to Africa forthwith.

I remember hearing them in Africa. It was a day of unrelenting heat, towards the end of the dry season in the Luangwa Valley in Zambia, with everyone longing for the rains. Then the sky clouded with reckless suddenness – it was as if the year had fast-forwarded three months in a quarter of an hour – and as this happened, high, high above, the faint sound of screaming. Turning binoculars skywards, it was just possible to make out the unmistakable sickle-shapes of a party of flying swifts: surfing in on the weather front. They looked as if they were towing the glorious gift of the rains behind them, and naturally, they were screaming at the tops of their voices.

This is not a hard sound to learn. But as you become a birdlistener, it becomes a sound that you will never, from this moment, ignore: one that will always reach you, one that will always bring you that touch of wildness even in the middle of a city.

And now your free gift

There are two ways of enjoying birdsong: two ways, for that matter, of enjoying the wild world. One is to take it as it comes, as part of the pattern of daily life; the other is to go out and look for it. Both are equally valid: both, so far as I am concerned, equally essential. Each comes with a built-in bonus: you are always likely to come across more than you bargained for. And that rule counts double once you have tuned your ears in as well as your eyes. You can, for example, go birding in complete darkness.

You can seek the wild world by choosing to take a walk: even by doing no more than choosing to sit out in the garden. You can then make a walk, an expedition – even a seated vigil, as I do for the swifts – with a target in mind, something you want to see, or want to hear. And the more you get your ear in, the more these esoteric pleasures come to matter.

I remember a Suffolk concert in deep darkness. It took place in late spring a couple of years ago. I had gone with my old friend John Burton, head honcho of the World Land Trust, an organisation that funds land purchase for wildlife conservation in all kinds of exciting areas of the world. We had gone to look for, or rather listen for, nightjars: mysterious birds of open country that earn their living by catching insects at night. Night is their time, and so, when they set up territories and seek mates, it's at night they do it. So we arrived after the late-spring dusk, and listened. And were gratified by the strange, unearthly chugging of the nightjar: a sound not only inhuman but unavian as well, unvertebral too, for that matter. There is a radiophonic tone to it, a twitching finger on the dial of a malfunctioning radio. It is a rich sound from a bird with a profoundly spooky tradition.

The place we had chosen was a patch of heathland maintained by the National Trust; its border marches along that of the RSPB's Minsmere nature reserve, forming a contiguous area of high-class habitat. So it was no overwhelming surprise that we then picked up the sound of bittern: the male uttering his foghorn boom from maybe as much as a mile away on this still evening.

A nightingale struck up. We shall look at nightingales in more detail later on, but here is a taster of this most extraordinary of all singers. Two or three males struck up. It was late in the season, their territories established, the business of breeding more than half done, so this was, by nightingale standards anyway, a somewhat per-functory effort. Never mind, it's never a bad thing to hear a nightingale, and these late-season fragments were a good reminder of just how fabulous this song can be.

Nor had the birds finished. Again from Minsmere, but not nearly so far off this time, another of those weird night birds: a stone curlew, the goggle-eyed screamer of dry and open country, lent its weird voice to the concert: an unexpected bonus, so much so that the voice, so very strange, had us stumped for a few moments until we remembered the phenomenal success they have had with these birds at Minsmere.

And still the night was not done with us. A strange trilling chatter came from the darkness: answered in the same way. And this time I was totally baffled. I hadn't even a good guess. But Burton cracked it almost at once: natterjack toad. A rare and difficult British amphibian, but one with a voice to remember.

So there it was: a wild wind quintet, a splendid recital a mile or so from the Suffolk coast: five wonderful, wild and seldom-heard creatures, all beasts that have much of their being in sound. The still night is their best time, when their voices will carry: each individual animal churring, booming, singing, screaming and croaking his identity out into the blackness of the Suffolk night.

There was a sense of privilege involved here. We were probably the only humans to be listening: the only humans able to enter into this world beyond humanity. Without having acquired the small talent for listening, we would have heard nothing but a strange din – but without it, we would not have been out there in the first place.

And that is the gift of this book. At least, I very much

hope so. You used to – perhaps you still do – get a free gift in a box of cereals: a plastic toy. Well, that's the free gift that comes with this book: a new sense. A sense of hearing, a sense of privilege, above all, a sense of belonging.

Seaside waders

The seaside will bring you more than seagulls. It will often bring the sound of other birds, birds you seldom hear inland. So here's a clue: if you hear a bird that's not a seagull anywhere around the coast, it's an oystercatcher. Well, that's a bit of an exaggeration, but it's a handy rule to begin with.

Oystercatcher

Oystercatchers seldom shut up. Any shrill piping or whistling noise, repeated with urgency approaching frenzy, is likely to be an oystercatcher. They send out far-carrying shrill trills, almost like a referee's whistle. When excited – and they seem to spend most of their lives excited – they will give a series of sounds like – and please excuse me as I break the pee-oo rule – k'peek k'peek k'peek.

It is pretty easy to get the hang of oystercatchers because they are also very visible birds: strongly black and white, with a beak like a carrot. You hear the distinctive call and you turn your eyes to see a distinctively marked bird that makes no effort to remain hidden. All birding ought to be like this. Oystercatchers are on your side.

Redshank

I'll give you three more waders to add to your beginner's pack, and they are all tremendously vocal. The redshank has perhaps the most pompous nickname among British birds: the sentinel of the marshes. If you take a walk anywhere squashy: along tidal mudflats or estuaries and coastal marshes, you will alarm the redshanks. Redshanks make it their business to be alarmed at the merest trifles. They are no stoics: when something disturbs, they take to the air and give a fine fluting triple-note of alarm, with a strong stress on the first syllable.

There are a great many variations in this, many of them used for less drastic purposes. If you sit still and listen to a distant group of wading birds, you will often hear redshanks calling to each other in a less frenzied fashion. They have a fine vocabulary of peeps and toots and whistles. This is a sound that is very much part of landscape: you will hear redshanks calling in the music of the Benjamin Britten opera *Peter Grimes*, which is set on the Suffolk coast. Their cry seems to be expressing the loneliness and the desolate nature of the uncompromising big-skied landscape, but for the birds themselves, it means nothing of the kind. The redshanks are expressing their solidarity with each other, and often expressing their contentment with the place they live in. It's all in the way you hear these things.

Curlew

The curlew is another bird associated with desolation. Its double-note call – the bird says its own name, generally stressing the final syllable – is almost always described as "haunting". In Thomas Gray's "Elegy in a Country Churchyard", "the curlew tolls the knell of parting day".

Curlews have a fair range of sounds, some based around those two syllables, repeated and varied. The most thrilling of their calls is the rich bubbling cry that carries for miles, sometimes repeated half a dozen times. Curlews can be found away from the coast too, on moors and uplands, where they breed.

Lapwing

Lapwings are not dogmatically coastal birds: they like most kinds of damp places. They have a strong and distinctive voice, and it is a good one to get logged in the mind. Lapwings are sometimes known as pewits, which gives a clue about the call. But the thing to remember is the reedy quality. Pewits sound just a little like oboes: double-reed instruments.

You can hear the basic pewit call in alarm, but as with the other waders, this is a theme that can have a lot of variations. If you listen to a flock, they will converse with each other in all kinds of subtle sounds. And when they move into display, they will work the basic call up into a frenzy, as they accompany themselves in a dizzy aerobatic performance.

These are all wading birds. There are an awful lot more of them, but you can investigate such things as Temminck's stint and the bar-tailed godwit in your own time. These four are intended to get you started with the long-legged birds; and as you get your ear in, you will at once discover that their voices are the finest and most atmospheric sounds you will encounter in a lifetime of birdlistening.

Hello

As you listen to the waders and the gulls, and learn to recognise them not from a single stereotyped call but from something much less specific, something more like the quality of voice, you must come to terms with the fact that birds are individuals. They are not just members of a species: every one alike, every one doing the same thing, every one responding in the same way. To say that a lapwing is a lapwing is not the end of the matter: certainly not for the lapwing.

Birds are not automata. You don't press a button and get a certain response. A redshank has an alarm call that is recognisably the call of a redshank. But as the bird makes this alarm call, he is also expressing a view on the nature and intensity of the threat: something that depends on context, on time of day, on the proximity of the threat, on the seriousness of the threat, and also, on the bird's own state of mind. A bird that has been seriously alarmed by a passing sparrowhawk will respond more radically to a passing walker than he would have done had he not just had a near miss with a dangerous predator.

At first listening, many birds seem to have a pretty

limited vocabulary: this sound for alarm, this for contact, this for display. But there is no hard-and-fast boundary between these things. A call can be varied in volume intensity, in rhythm, in repetition. After all, a human can say hello in dozens of different ways. It's always a greeting, but there are all kinds of subtle variations. Let's say you're taking a call on your mobile phone: a name comes up on the screen and you say hello. You can say it with indifference, with amiability, with hostility; you can say it flirtily; you can say it with the deepest love of which you are capable. Hello is just a contact call, but it has many different meanings and many different implications.

Birds use their voices to express important concepts. And as you begin to listen, you begin to get a closer understanding of what they mean. As you do so, you are letting your understanding of the world reach out beyond the barrier of species. That is something everyone with a cat or a dog or a horse is able to do, in spite of the fact that many philosophers have told us that this is impossible. A dog owner can tell his own dog's state of mind from a bark; a birdlistener can understand all kinds of intriguing things from the immense and subtle variations of the simplest calls all around.

The beauty of it is that this is something that goes beyond book-learning. A book can't explain the difference between the please-let-me-in bark, the cat-in-the-garden bark and the bark that means there's a human intruder. And you can't learn about the subtle variations in the sounds of birds by listening to recordings. You acquire this knowledge more or less without conscious effort, just by subliminal awareness, by becoming a birdlistener. As you do so, you slowly become aware that the process has made the world a good deal richer.

Crows

Crows call all through the year. It's not pretty. Few people learn birdsong so that they can listen to crows. All the same, crows have their points. They are highly intelligent. I visited Professor Nicky Clayton in her aviary at Cambridge University, where she has demonstrated that in every respect, crows are the intellectual equals of chimpanzees. Crows are immensely resourceful birds and most of the many crow species worldwide are extremely adept at exploiting humans.

They are not great on melody. That has to be admitted. But the sounds they make are important as we reach an understanding of the life of wild birds and what's happening in it. They provide a kind of percussion section – perhaps more so than the woopeckers – with a range of harsh and sometimes challenging sounds. If you prefer, they provide the punctuation to the narrative of birdsong.

We'll start with the crow that's usually just called a crow. There are three black crows commonly found in this country, and the non-technical tend to call them all crows. Birders tend to refer to them collectively as corvids, to make it clear that they are talking about more than one species. Crow tends to mean carrion crow: one large black species, a member of the crow family.

Carrion crow

Carrion crows say crow. Or caw or kraw or kraaaagh, or however you care to write it. It's a strong, fierce sound: angry-sounding, some like to say. It tends to come in triplets: three angry caws in rapid succession mean a carrion crow. You mostly find carrion crows in pairs, sometimes as singletons, so when you hear a mass outbreak of cawing, it is less likely to be carrion crows than rooks. But this is not a hard-and-fast rule: "One rooks is crows, two crows is rooks" is the right idea, but it's only a guideline. Carrion crows will sometimes make flocks and sometimes join in flocks with rooks and jackdaws. But their caw is always different, even if sometimes it's difficult to be certain.

Rook

Rooks have their being in togetherness. They also love to caw. They adore cawing: they do it all the time. They don't caw in triplets, and their caw has a much mellower tone. Rooks don't sound angry: they sound rather pleased with life, on the whole. And when they are together, as they usually are, they talk to each other all the time.

The rook vocabulary goes a good way beyond caw. They are also prone to squeaks and pops and barks and yelps and strange bugling notes. Their commonplace appearance and their unprepossessing faces – they seem to be all beak, and that beak the colour of old bones – tend to distract us humans from the fact that they have a complex life based around an intriguing system of communication. As a result of the time I spent with Professor Clayton, I found myself looking more closely at wild crow flocks after she had shown me the faithfulness of the rook couples in her aviary. If you watch rooks, you can pick out an individual and usually establish that he or she is doing everything with strict reference to one other. Cawing and squeaking and bugling as the lifelong pair-bond is constantly maintained in the affectionate hurly-burly of the flock.

Jackdaw

The third black crow is the jackdaw. And it doesn't say crow, it says jack. There is a range of variations and subtleties in this, as you would expect from an intelligent and social species, but it is that jack that rings out, and it is utterly distinctive. You can hear it from pairs and singletons; you can hear it in loose gatherings of a dozen or so; you can hear it in large flocks. One of the great sounds of lowland Britain is the great flocks of mixed corvids, which are generally rooks and jackdaws, but often with a few carrion crows thrown in. The dominant sound is the mellow cawing of the rooks, echoed and repeated and re-echoed, against the staccato background of the explosive jacks – all with a subtle garnish of the rooks' bugling notes.

Bleeding obvious

Birds speak, but is it language? Animals of all kinds communicate with each other in many different ways, but does any of it actually count as language? The answers given to these questions may not tell us very much about animals, but they do tell us quite a bit about what kind of human beings we are. On one side, there are people who are eager – perhaps over-eager – to stress the continuity between humans and other forms of life. And on the other, there are people who are eager, to the point of desperation, to demonstrate that humans are completely different from all other lifeforms.

There are many complex philosophical definitions of what language is. Some would say that one of the most important things about human language is that we can use it to have meaningful communication about something that is physically absent. But the waggle-dance of the bees – when one worker bee shows the others where to find a rich nectar source – does precisely that, so bang goes that notion as a way of separating humans from all other fellow-animals.

There are other ideas about what constitutes a language. The attachment of arbitrary sounds to a real meaning, for example: the word "bird" doesn't sound like a bird. Language works by being passed on from one individual to another, that is to say, it's a matter of culture. Some maintain that animals are incapable of any form of cultural transmission. Some say that the crucial point is that language can be used to discuss language, precisely as I am trying to do here.

But all these definitions seem to me to be not so much arguments as barriers. If we demonstrate that – and this has been done many times, though seldom unchallenged – non-humans really do have something that can be called a culture, then some counter-arguers will redefine culture, and claim that this new definition demonstrates for all time that there is an uncrossable barrier between humans and everything else that ever lived. This insistence that only humans have language seems to involve skewing the definition of language, so that it covers stuff that only humans can do. In other words, it only counts as a language if humans can do it: not the most stimulating way of thinking. This tendency reminds me of the way we used to measure intelligence. Early in the 20th century, all kinds of ingenious scientific labour created unanswerable demonstrations that white people were innately smarter than black people – and all this stuff was subsequently exploded, not by political correctness but by science.

For me, these philosophical questions about language are interesting for anyone who uses language – but ultimately unhelpful when it comes to thinking about non-human animals. Humans communicate. Non-human animals communicate. Is there a magic moment when the complex chattering of rooks in a rookery becomes language, or when a dolphin's clicks and whirrs reach the same point of dignity? Was there an instant when the chattering of proto-humans became the language of human beings? Absurd. You might just as well argue about the magic moment when a stream becomes a river. A river is, unquestionably and incontrovertibly, a river: and the same is true for a stream. But there is no single instant when the two are obviously and for all time separate things.

Basil Fawlty says that his wife Sybil's specialist subject on *Mastermind* would be "the bleeding obvious". Here are two points that both come from the area of the bleeding obvious. The first is that humans are different from other animals in very many ways. The second is that humans *are* other animals. There is a continuum between humans and the wild world. We are so closely related to chimpanzees and bonobos that some who study the complex questions of taxonomy suggest that one of two matters needs to be done if we are to understand the nature of primates and the place of humans in the natural order. The first is to classify humans as chimpanzees; the second is to classify chimpanzees as hominids.

The history of humankind has been one of flight from the wild world. We have done everything we possibly could to prove to our own satisfaction that we have nothing whatsoever to do with other animals. Our entire civilisation is built on this premise. It is therefore deeply disturbing to consider that we are part of the same continuum as dolphins, apes, and for that matter, the birds and bees. Developed language is one of our genuine differences: but at bottom, we are all animals who communicate with each other, just like the rooks in the rookery and the redshanks out on the marsh.

The more you look at the natural world, the more you see that there are very few hard-and-fast barriers. You share a common ancestor with your goldfish and with the oak tree in the park. Like birds, you communicate. As you become a birdlistener, you will increasingly find, along with the beginnings of understanding, the acceptance of kinship.

Two more crows

We had better clear up two more members of the crow family: two birds that make sounds often heard throughout the year.

Magpie

Let us start with the magpie: a staccato cackle that has attracted a number of unflattering descriptions. The Chinese say it sounds like someone shaking a bagfull of money. Gerald Durrell said that his pet magpies – the Magenpies – used to torment the chickens next door by imitating the sound that summoned them to food, after which they would "chuckle like a pair of city slickers that have successfully duped a crowd of bumbling

and earnest villagers". Magpies have a sinister reputation for theft and for other terrible crimes. They are visually prominent and much disliked. Once you get your ears tuned in to birdsong, you will be able to put to bed one of the great magpie legends: that if you have magpies around, you won't get any songbirds, because the magpies eat all the songbird nestlings. You hear and see magpies about the place, but as you learn to listen to birdsong, you will hear that there is a great deal of it going on even while the magpies cackle. The extinction of songbirds at the beaks of magpies is a myth that anyone with ears can expose.

Their most frequent call is a sharp, rather wooden-sounding rattle, very distinctive and obvious once you've got the hang of it. Even if you haven't consciously associated the sound with magpies, you will know it as soon as you hear it. They also make other, more subtle sounds, with clicks and squeaks, but the rattle is the sound that means magpie.

Jay

Jays are also crows, and if that seems surprising in a bird that carries feathers of pink and iridescent blue, one look at the beak and the knowing eye will tell you that these are proper crows. Professor Nicky Clayton of Cambridge found that her aviary jays are remarkable problem-solvers. If you float a juicy meal worm in a glass of water too narrow to allow the bird to grab it with its beak, it will drop stones into the glass to raise the water level, and with it, the worm. Give them false stones that will float instead of sink, and they will ignore them and go straight to the identically coloured real stones.

It has to be said that their principal sound does not reflect this great intelligence. Jays scream. If you are in a wood and hear the most ungodly racket you have ever heard in your life, it's a jay. When alarmed, generally by you and often at long distance, they will let rip a great rasping scream. It has been described as the violent ripping of a taut fabric: a great cloth-ripping screech.

Jays, like magpies, have other sounds and subtler expressions, but it is the screech that is their stand-out call. Stop for a moment when you hear it, and you may well see the serrated wings and the bewildering colours of a bird that has been called "the British bird of paradise". You'll find them in most places where there are oak trees; they're great acorn eaters. They will often tell you they are about: and do so at deafening volume.

World Cup birding

There are too many species in the world. Too many, that is, for us to understand easily. It is rather like the World Cup finals. In the old days – like when England won the damn thing in 1966 – there were only 16 teams at the finals, so it was quite an easy business to see most of the teams and the players, and to get some kind of understanding of the way they operated, their strength and weakness and their chances of winning the tournament. As a result, you could get some grasp of the universals: of the central principles that governed the dynamic of the tournament. But these days, there are 32 teams, three matches every day during the early stages, and nobody has the time to watch them all. So we have a paradox: the more nations there are at the World Cup, the less we understand the variousness and vastness of the event. Instead, we reduce it to something we can easily understand. For most people in England, there is England, and there is abroad. There is us, and there are them. It all comes down to one question: will England win? And the nation, apart from dedicated football enthusiasts, is content – eager – to leave it at that. Either England wins or Abroad wins. Such contests as

Paraguay v South Korea do not trouble us very greatly. The World Cup has become binary.

The overwhelming nature of the biodiversity of the earth has produced the same effect. There are so many other kinds of living thing that we tend to see life in binary terms. Us and them. Humans and animals. It is much easier that way. There are, as we know, about 10,000 species of bird in the world, and just about all of them make noises of different kinds. I say "about" 10,000 species because no one ever knows the precise number. It is always changing. Scientists are always deciding that these two slightly different populations are in fact members of the same species, or that these two slightly different populations are in fact two good species. When it was agreed that the Scottish crossbill was a different species to the crossbill, many list-keeping birders were delighted to find that they had a new bird on their lists without having to leave the house: an armchair tick, in the jargon.

The more interesting question is about why there are so many different kinds of bird. The great mystery of life is not why we are here, but how come there are so many of us, so many different kinds of us living things.

This truth about the teeming nature of the world is a hard one to deal with: a bit like trying to read Stephen Hawking. It's so much simpler to revert to the binary us-and-them notion. But the more you listen to birds, the more you find this simple antithetical model of the universe unsatisfying. The urge to revel in our – quite

SIMON BARNES

genuine – human uniqueness becomes subtly under-
mined by an equal and opposite urge to savour our part
in the continuum of life: to seek comfort and meaning
in our connectedness. It's a contradiction: and in that
contradiction lies our humanity.

Freshwater birds

If you find yourself by a decent stretch of fresh water, you will hear different birds to those you heard in the woods, or for that matter, by the sea. There is some overlap between sea and inland waters – black-headed gulls, most obviously – but there is a different soundscape.

Mallard

Quack. That's one you knew. Duck, or to be precise, mallard, the commonest duck in this country. Or to be even more precise, the female mallard. The quack of the male is lower and different in quality. The female will often give a series of quacks, fading away towards the end, in a sound a little like maniacal laughter.

Moorhen

You will often hear moorhens calling from cover at the edge of ponds and lakes: a sort of contralto squeak with a trilled R. Moorhens are not particularly wary birds, but they spend a large amount of time foraging in cover; they are able climbers and clamberers. You will often hear them when they are out of sight, when they are walking round or near fresh water, usually close to the edge. If you are in such places at twilight, or even in full darkness, you will often hear a moorhen calling out. The call can be subtly varied, but it always has the same moorhen flavour.

Coot

Coots are closely related to moorhens – they are both rails – but they like to stress their differences. This is apparent not only from beak and face colours – coot white, moorhen red – but also in their calls. The coots don't trill: they give a clear, rather popping call. Helpfully enough, they say coot. While moorhens like the edges and the shallows, coots prefer the middle and the deep water, and are efficient divers. Coots like to be together, but they also have a well-developed taste for a punch-up. They go in for loud splashing and coot-cooting chases.

There are plenty of other intriguing sounds to hear around fresh water, but I'll leave them for you to discover as you get your ear in. There are some great duck noises – the whistling of wigeon is a favourite with everyone who likes birds – but I don't want to deafen you with science. Leave those as treats to discover in the fullness of time. But a couple more freshwater sounds will be useful.

Heron

Herons bark. When you hear a rough, rather raucous, and usually monosyllabic shout, lift your eyes and you will see a heron cruising in on big arched wings. They will also bark when disturbed – an alarm call that sounds rather like a rude word thrown over their shoulders as they withdraw.

Dabchick

There's another sound that I'll include here because it so often dismays the beginner birdlistener. It certainly dismayed the hell out of me until I cracked it. The bird that makes it is more or less the last bird you'd expect. You'll hear it mostly in spring, and generally from cover at the edge of the water: ponds, lakes and ditches. It is a far-carrying tittering trill: a musical giggling. And as you wonder what hidden warbler would be making this pleasing little call, a dabchick swims past. Don't carry on looking for the warbler: the dabchick, sometimes called the little grebe, is the titterer.

But does it really count?

List, list, oh list! The ghost's command to Hamlet. Meaning listen, rather than write down all the birds you've seen today. This book is all about listing, in the sense of listening – though I'm not planning to tell you a tale whose lightest word would harrow up your soul, freeze your young blood and make your knotted and combined locks to part and each particular hair stand on end like quills upon the fretful porpentine.

But what about listing, in the more usual birding sense of the term?

The first point is that lists are not compulsory. Certainly, many birders keep lists, and many of these see list-making as a token of their seriousness. But it's not essential to the pursuit of birds and birding. A list is something that reduces your day, your trip, your year, or your life to a number. That can be revealing in terms of biodiversity, or in terms of the expertise of the birder. It can also reveal the lister's energy, or for that matter, the depth of his pockets. For some, keeping the score is important, even essential. For others, not at all. It's a question of whether you wish your birding to be spiced up with the Tabasco of sport. That's simply a matter of personal taste and nothing more. I put Tabasco on chips; I don't keep lists.

The twitchers love the hot taste of sport, and that's all fine and dandy. But they sometimes forget that twitching is not all and everything to do with birding. All twitchers are birders, but by no means all birders are twitchers. Twitchers are the hard-core listers who not only keep the score but regularly travel miles to see a windblown rarity. They get a good deal of their pleasure from birds by this competitive listing. But many other birders prefer to work a local patch. And many, many others – among them myself – enjoy birds in a much less structured way. Some twitchers might say, a less committed way, though I would dispute that. I'm committed to birds all right. I'm not so desperately committed to watching them, recording them and making lists of them, but I am profoundly committed to the joy birds can bring and the conservation movement that birds need if they are to carry on surviving and singing. Make lists if the practice gives you pleasure. But not making lists doesn't mean you're not a birder, or even a lesser birder. Birds give joy to all who turn eyes and ears towards them.

Old birder's conundrum, one that particularly vexes the twitching tendency: can you count a bird if you've only heard it? To this I respond: what do you mean, "only"? Why should you count a bird if you've "only" seen it?

What's all this about the primacy of sight? It takes us back to the argument of the sixth-form common room: would you sooner be blind or deaf? It has been suggested that the reason we think sight is so important is because of written language. The invention of writing, and the imparting and storing of important information in written form, made us value sight more than any other sense. We generally refer to the pre-literate world as an oral culture, meaning also an aural culture. In these cultures, important matters were transmitted by sound and therefore received by ear. A pre-literate culture would probably have viewed (another seeing word, but that's the nature of our language) hearing as the primary sense. And that, I think, explains something about the pleasures of birdlistening: it takes us away from our civilised selves and back to a time when hearing was as important, if not more important than seeing. Listening, as we have already discussed, was an important part of staying alive: it was also the most important part of understanding our fellow-humans, our fellow-creatures, and the environment we all shared. If we learn how to listen to the wild world as well as look at it, we will understand our own environment more profoundly, and relish that sense of completion that comes from the rediscovery of links with our ancestral past.

My answer to the question of counting a bird that is "only" heard is an unequivocal yes. Jeremy Mynott, in his fine book *Birdscapes*, says: "The only thing interesting about the question is that it should arise at all." If you are doing an ornithological survey of a piece of land, you don't wait until you have seen a bird before entering it on your map. Very often, your ears have already told you what bird you have encountered. There is no question of doubt. I have done it myself: I remember surveying a farm on which I recorded five turtle doves. They were unquestionably turtle doves. They could not possibly have been anything else. So I wrote them down, thereby demonstrating that the farmer was doing a very decent job for conservation.

There can be problems in working by ear. A lot of calls overlap, so you need to use common sense. You don't guess. The songs of garden warbler and blackcap – as we shall see in due course – are notoriously open to confusion; and in this case, surveyors of uncertain expertise are sometimes requested to try and see the bird before making their diagnosis. But a clear and unambiguous burst of song or an unmistakable call from any species means that you have recorded a species of bird with perfect accuracy. Me, I seldom even seek out willow warblers or nightingales with my eyes. They are drab birds that call from thick vegetation, but they have great and glorious songs that tell me all I want to know about them. The sound of a bittern foghorning from the reeds doesn't inspire me to go crashing through the reed-bed until I have disturbed him and put him to flight. It's just a wonderful sound to hear, especially at dawn with the mist beginning to burn off, and that's more than good enough for me. I know it's a bittern, I'm glad it's a bittern, I'd tell anyone it's a bittern, I'd write it down as a bittern, and if I kept a list, I'd list it as a bittern.

So yes: birdlistening is proper birding. And it's not a secondary pleasure either: for me it's a primary one. I wouldn't trouble to separate the senses: sight and sound are all part of the greater experience of being out there in a wild place, feeling the mist in the air and the sun on your back, with the scent of the mud in your nostrils and the taste of breakfast to come.

If you wish to list, then list, oh list – but count the birds you listen to as well as those you see. Clapping your ears on a bird is just as valid, and often a great deal more rewarding than just clapping your eyes on one.

Geese

We'd better not leave fresh water without listening to a goose or two. There are two common species, encountered throughout the year, whose unmelodic voices can be heard around lakes and rivers. You also find them on and around fields within striking distance of water – geese are great grazers and must consume an awful lot of grass, because they don't get much nutrition from it. As a result, they are always grazing and leaving behind copious traces of their grazing – the phrase "loose as a goose" is not there just for the rhyme – to the great irritation of people who use playing-fields close to rivers.

Greylag goose

The greylag goose is brown with a big orange beak, and it is the ancestor of farmyard geese just as the mallard is the ancestor of farmyard ducks. You will often see farmyard geese, or wild/domestic hybrids among greylag flocks. Geese are social creatures, and voice is an important ingredient in the glue that keeps the flocks together. They tend to give out big, loud monosyllabic honks at important moments, like when a flock takes off or lands, or when outlying geese join up with the main flock. There is a fair amount of variation within the basic honk, and other quieter, more conversational sounds. There is a nasal quality to the honk. The birds are pretty visible, but when silhouetted with the sun behind them, or when hidden behind reeds, or at distance across a field, the voice can separate them from other geese.

Canada goose

The other common goose to look out for is the Canada goose, a bird not much liked, particularly by rugby players, being great grazers of playing fields. They are rather resented by many people as foreign interlopers with a foreign name: they were first brought to England to please the owners of large aristocratic estates, but they got out and spread. They make a familiar sight, striking-looking birds, and their voice is almost as familiar.

Unlike the greylags, the Canadas give a two-syllable honk. The first syllable is almost a hum, with a slightly clarinet-ish tone to it: they will use this syllable on its own in quieter conversations among themselves when on the ground. But with a full-on honk, they move away from the woodwind section and trumpet with a great brassy note that's higher in pitch. For North American birders, it's a sound full of atmosphere and memories of dawn vigils across marshes as great skeins of these strong and handsome birds set off on migration. But in this country, they are merely regarded as noisy buggers, and foreigners to boot.

I rather admire the way they have made an unfamiliar place work so well for them. They don't bother to migrate here, but they are prone to cross-country journeys, always in the that V-shaped skein essential for goose transit, constantly double-honking at each other as they go, encouraging each other to keep the formation tight and to take turns at the toughest position at the head of the skein.

I quite like them because sometimes, often during the winter, on a train journey, or in a town, you will hear the stirring double honk, lift your eyes and see a skein of them flying from one reservoir to another. And if you have a short winter's day all taken up with business under roofs, it will probably be the most inspiring thing you see and hear all day.

Song of the butterfly

It's high summer, and the birder's thoughts tend to turn to – well, they tend to turn to butterflies, these days. Some of the better observers turn to dragonflies. This versatility is something of a new thing among birders, and it came about because in the high summer, it all goes quiet. That's literally true: birds really don't make much noise during the warmest months.

There's good reason for this. Breeding territories have been set up, mates have been won, eggs have been laid, young have hatched. As the breeding season wears on, it becomes counter-productive to make too much noise. For those birds that have a second brood, often the advertisement for the territory is more perfunctory. The hard work has, after all, already been done. The local population of rivals know you are there: your main job's been achieved.

And then, as the summer continues, many of the songbirds finish their breeding programme and go into a moult. That means they change all their feathers. This doesn't happen all at once – a naked and flightless bird wouldn't survive terribly long – but over the course of a few weeks. For the small insect-eaters like blue tits, this will take about six weeks; a couple of weeks longer for seed-eaters like the finches. This is because insect-eating birds obtain keratin – the stuff from which feathers (and for that matter, your hair and fingernails) are made – from insects. In this period, the moulting birds are vulnerable, and so it makes sense to keep quiet, to keep hunkered down until the next big thing happens – which tends to be the autumn.

This quiet period doesn't mean there is no point in birding: only that birds are harder to find, and that your listening skills are put to a more searching test. You will hear more small, subtle calls than full-out songs. So enjoy the warm weather, the intriguing nature of the summer hideaway – and of course, it's a great time to expand your horizons. Butterflies and dragonflies are great, and I love to look for and at them, and all forms of life are rich and rewarding – but they are beyond my remit here. After all, they don't sing very much.

Birds of prey

As the summer moves on and the rhythm of the year changes, so the soundscape changes with it. The birds of prey take longer than the little songbirds to rear a nestful of young, and they don't go in for multiple broods. And sometimes, as the breeding season winds down to a close, you bump into young birds of prey, and it can be a mightily cheering experience.

Kestrel

Young kestrels fledge and learn how to fly, but are still dependent on their parents for food. So they will get up to all kinds of hooligan antics around the nest site. My father sees them as young toughs from *West Side Story*, singing "When you're a kes you're a kes". They play mad chasing games, learning in play how to use their wings and their judgement, skills that will be vital to them in adult life. And as they do so, they make a serious din.

The pee-oo rule must be broken again here: just about everybody agrees that what the birds says is kikiki, or ki-ki-ki. This doesn't necessarily come in triplets: it is a rapid series of high screaming notes: birds of prey tend to go in for wild high cries, not the basso roars you might expect from creatures of such ferocity. Adult birds are much less vocal, though all birds of prey will utter shrill and excited calls at mating time. The sound of the kestrel is most often heard as a celebration of young life, and a sign that the breeding season for just about every bird is now an accomplished fact rather than an ongoing process. The aeronautical display that accompanies this wild kikiki-ing chorus is one the great sights in British birding.

Sparrowhawk

It's possible that when walking through a wood at this time of year you might hear the sound of a cat stuck up a tree. Stop and listen. It now sounds like three, maybe four cats, all stuck up different trees in close vicinity. Don't investigate too closely, because you don't want to disturb them. These are young sparrowhawks making their hunger calls. They are big enough to make loud noises and to move about the wood a little, but they still need food from their parents.

This is not a sound you are going to hear every day, or even every year, but it's a splendid event when you come across it, and I feel I should tell you about it here – not least because it is a real puzzler if you can't crack it. Again, it's a vivid sound that tells of the turning of the year.

Buzzard

While we are on the subject of big fierce birds, I had better include buzzard, the most gabby of all birds of prey. Readers from the West Country, if they have even the slightest interest in birds, are likely to be familiar with the sound of buzzards: indeed, many West Country people would put down buzzard as one of the birdsound sthey knew already, as unmistakable as a quacking duck and a cuckooing cuckoo.

Buzzards are spreading out from their stronghold in the west, and they can be heard, outside towns, in most parts of Britain these days. But in the west they are a daily sight and sound. The basic call is a wild mewing, though it's more crazy and more monstrous than a cat. The place that the call comes from is a bit of a giveaway: the sky. Buzzards are great soarers and gliders and they are often very noisy on the wing. If you hear a mad cat calling from a clear sky, you've found a buzzard. As the breeding season closes, you may hear young birds, whose hunger calls are far-carrying and rather gull-like.

Silence

There is another sound that will enrich you very much once you start to listen to birds.

Silence

We live in a world of din. I used to live in Hong Kong, one of the world's noisiest cities. For a few weeks after I arrived, I lived in the middle of town. When I went out into the countryside, to the outlying islands and into what were then the New Territories, I felt the absence of traffic noise so strongly that I literally felt dizzy. The balancing mechanism for our bodies is located in the inner ear, and I suppose some confused message about this radical change in the ears created this sense of dis orientation. After several of these experiences, I moved out onto one of the outlying islands myself.

Wherever we live, din follows us around, and we learn to tune it out. We do this in pubs with background music, until, of course, they start to play your song. Traffic noise is all around, piped music follows us, peaceful Sunday afternoons are filled with the sounds of lawn mowers and strimmers and next-door's television. We protect ourselves from the loneliness of silence by means of man-made din. So much so that we hardly notice it: we live in a cocoon of sound, an ear-filling environment in which there is always some kind of noise to remind us that we are humans and we are safe from the wild world. When I visit London, I am passed and repassed by joggers and cyclists, going by with a desperate pant and with the white plugs of their iPods in their ears.

But I am not here to give you a rant about the follies and evils of our civilisation. No: this whole book is an invitation to escape some of the demands of noise. If you get into the habit of listening to birds, you start to become more aware of many other sounds as well. The buzzing of bees and insects; the stridulation of crickets and grasshoppers; the sound of wind in the leaves or in the seed-heads of a reed-bed; the waves of the sea and the shifting of the shingle beneath. You hear them because you have tuned in your ears.

I love looking at birds, and I carry a notebook and occasionally even write things down in it. I carry a pair of rather good binoculars; sometimes I carry two pairs, one for ultra-close-focus work with invertebrates. (If that sounds a bit serious and committed, please understand that what I really mean is going "wow" at close-up views of butterflies, occasionally actually identifying them.) When I first got used to listening to birds, I wondered about adding to my equipment. I thought about recording birdsong. There are all kinds of groovy pieces of gear you can buy, and that's a fun concept right from the start. I knew that recording birdsong would make me listen more and stay out longer.

My old friend Bob is a great recorder of birds, and has made it his life's work to record the sounds of the birds of Zambia. He did much of his pioneering work with a reel-to-reel tape recorder, an omni-directional microphone and a parabolic reflector he made himself. I have been on bird-recording trips with him, mostly in Africa, but on one rather splendid May dawn, we recorded an hour-long duet between bittern and nightingale, perched as we were between reed-bed and spinney in Suffolk.

But in the end I decided against, and I did so for reasons of silence. Bird-recorders always seek purity. The recordings that accompany this book have been selected because of their lack of distracting background din. As a result of the quest for purity, there is a danger that you spend your time listening not to the birds, but at the passing aeroplanes, distant cars, barking dogs, whining power tools and cheery farmers giving you the traditional country greeting.

Silence is rarely pure. You can hear real silence sometimes deep in a cave – when, if you stop talking, the sound of nothing comes as a physical shock. But away from the cities, sometimes even away from the hum of traffic, you can get closer to silence. Silence is never complete, but you can get closer to it because the human brain helps you out – so long as you are not making a recording of birdsong. Your brain is very good at filtering out unwanted sounds, as you know from sitting in that music-filled pub or walking through a busy street. That means you can get closer to a perceived silence as a birdlistener moving out into the wild world – especially if you have no recording equipment, and the awareness of every little sound that goes with it.

So the birdlistener gets more than most other travellers in wild places: an appreciation not only of the natural sounds around – running water in the stream; the sound of your feet on the path; the crackle of vegetation as you brush past – but also a positive and conscious appreciation of the lack of man-made noise. This, you will soon find, is a much stronger experience than you would expect from a mere absence. This comparative silence is a positive thing: it implies not the absence of human things, but the presence of wild ones.

It might even be that if you use this book to become a birdlistener, then the greatest gift this book will have brought you is silence.

Owls

As the breeding season ends and young birds leave the nest to go and seek their fortune, the normal pattern of life is disrupted for the owls. As a result, the owls are at their noisiest. Many species of owl tend to be fixtures in a place: once they have settled on a territory, they stay there not only throughout the year but for the rest of their lives. This can make it tough for the ambitious youngster, who leaves the nest and tries to find a territory for himself. And he does so by making a noise – and that noise will produce a furious and noisy response if there is already an owl there.

Sometimes a major debate between intruder and incumbent will spread out into other species of owl: excited by the sounds of vocal conflict, they raise their own voices in sympathy. I have heard, from my own house, a discussion of the facts of life between three species of owl, tawny, barn and little, with as many as a dozen birds involved.

Many species of owl keep up a territory all year, so they are likely to call all year, but as summer moves into autumn, you hear them at their gabbiest. So let's start with the tawny owl: the owl that was there at the beginning of the book as one of the birds whose voices you already knew.

Tawny owl

A tawny owl doesn't go tu-wit tu-woo. It goes tu-wit *and* it goes tu-woo. The tu-woo is the familiar sound: the sound you hear every time there is a graveyard in a film. It's not strictly two syllables: it will often hoot with a single syllable, and then follow with a more wavering hoot, with half a dozen wobbles in it. They are the most nocturnal of owls. Other owls like dawn and dusk, and the short-eared owl is regularly seen working in daylight. But tawny owls really do like the deep dark, and they will hoot from pitch darkness, which gives them their sinister reputation. They will call from mature trees: they like thick woodland but will also use copses and hedgerows with mature trees, and they will move from one to the other on regular hunting patrols. They will defend these places with their hoots.

The tu-wit sound is a contact call: often a way for male and female to keep in touch across their shared territory in the darkness. Both sexes use it: it has often been suggested that the female says tu-wit and the male says tu–woo, but both sexes use both calls, and various subtle variations around them.

Barn owl

I will touch briefly on two other vocal species of owl, because knowing them will enrich your life if you take a country walk at dusk. Barn owls will often call in these transitional times. You will hear them in open country: they like to work rough grassland and the margins of fields, following the hedge-lines like giant white moths. They make an utterly disconcerting hissing screech, one of the most chilling sounds you will hear from a British bird. That's because it doesn't really sound like a bird: it sounds like some sinister creature from our imaginations welcoming the night with a ghastly sound. Barn owls have local names of screech owl, hissing owl, screaming owl and roarer. For a birdlistener, at least some of the sinister connotations of this sound and this bird melt away as you listen, and you feel not fear and dismay, but delight that so spectacular a bird – as remarkable in appearance as in voice – should be around and sharing the same bit of countryside as yourself. Knowing birds turns fear into joy.

Little owl

Little owls love to make a noise. They were introduced to this country, like Canada geese, but they are one invading bird that never gets any hate mail. They are a delight to everyone. Like barn owls, they like dusk best for making a din, but they will call any time, from darkness and in the middle of the day. Their most characteristic sound is somewhere between a deep whistle and a yelp, the yelping part like a little ratty dog, and it is used for contact and for alarm, varying in intensity and frequency. The male will give a territorial hoot, a calmer and less yelpy version of the alarm call: a deep whistle without the doggy bit.

Winter thrushes

The summer moult is over. The summer migrants have finished breeding and are on their way back south again. As autumn becomes established and winter follows, you can count yourself a second-winter birdlistener. That means that when the robins, newly moulted, set up their winter feeding territories, you know all about it, because you recognise their song, and – even though it means winter is upon you – you welcome the song for the sake of the singers and for your own delight in being able to recognise them. Confirmed birdlistener as you now are, you have become a participant in the turning of the year.

On fine days you hear a wren and a dunnock, and you are often aware of a bird party convened by the long-tailed tits, something you know about from the busy calling above your head. The sharp call of the great spotted woodpecker makes you look up to catch the switchbacking birds as they commute from tree to tree.

And because you are now a birdlistener, you begin to notice other calls. Calls you hadn't heard before, neither in the busy spring of your first year of learning, nor in the quieter summer that followed. And sometimes, this bird is genuinely new to you: migrant birds who come to us for the winter. They come to escape the harshness of Scandinavian winters, just as willow warblers escape the cold of our own winter by flying beyond the Sahara.

Fieldfare

There are two species of winter thrush, two thrushes that spend the colder months with us. They can be seen in ones and twos, but they are more often found in flocks. Fieldfares are handsome birds, most easily identified by sight when they fly away and show us their black tails. But usually you have identified them already because of the quacking sound they make. They make it most of the time: they like to keep in contact with each other. They often quack in triplets, sometimes monosyllabically, sometimes they string a good few together to express special moments of excitement. The sound is duck-like enough to be a helpful way of remembering them, even if it is not something you would ever confuse with a real duck. You hear them calling from the sky as they pass over, in trees where they roost, on the ground in open spaces where they feed.

Redwing

The other winter thrush is the redwing. In October, you will hear a high, thin call from overhead, sometimes with a trill in it. The redwings are coming, and bringing winter with them. They will hang about until the spring calls them north again. And when the redwings are on the move, it is time to start preparing for your second spring as a birdlistener.

Second Spring

Birds and Venice

And so it begins again. As spring begins to exert its grip, you hear a strident two-note call and – well, it's not the way it was the previous spring, is it? Firstly, you know it's a great tit as soon as you hear it, and secondly, you were listening out for it. You heard it distinctly, not as part of the background babble. You heard it as a great tit, not as some generalised mush of birdsong. Your ears are now tuned into the wild world. You are aware of the meaning of birdsong, because you are able to identify the voices of individual species. You are aware of the phenomenon of spring as never before, because you are able to isolate individual species from the chorus. In this second spring, you will understand that listening to birds has not just made you a better birder: it has enriched your life on many other levels.

I remember my second spring as a birdlistener. As a fully – or at least a partially – fledged birdlistener. The splendid double: familiarity with the birds I remembered from the previous year, and the still more thrilling ability to isolate the birds that I didn't know.

Perhaps I should make that clearer. If you hear a birdsong you don't know, your ignorance now has a new and very positive meaning. It probably means that you have picked out another species. It means that your ears are now good enough to distinguish between familiar and unfamiliar. This is pleasing in itself. It is also pleasing in the pleasure that awareness of biodiversity always deals out. And it is also pleasing because you can look up this new and unfamiliar bird and learn it and so add it to your vocabulary.

You will also find a small miracle. Spring is now coming to you earlier. You are now noticing when the brave pioneer birds raise their voices in defiance of the chill of the early few weeks of the year. You will find that your familiarity with wrens and dunnocks and great tits gives the spring an added urgency: you are becoming more than an observer; you are taking part in the drama of spring.

And so you listen more. The stuff you learned over the previous spring has given you a basic structure: with this, you can feel emboldened to listen in a deeper and more meaningful fashion. You find yourself listening to the songs themselves: not just in order to identify a bird, but for the pleasure of the song itself.

The song thrush cuts in, with his improvisations and his repetitions, and his careless raptures sung twice over and again once more. And you find yourself listening with a deeper appreciation: perhaps even a deeper understanding. You will appreciate his versatility, and without going into the heady science of it all, you will be aware, as never before, of the scope and range that a song thrush can attain.

So now I propose to take you through your second spring as a birdlistener. Sometimes, when you visit a place for the first time, it is wonderful, but then again it is almost too much. A place like Venice blows you away: the absurd magnificence of the Grand Canal, the overwhelming art, the drama of the Piazza, the gloriously sinister back alleys. You can't cope with it all: it comes as a wonderfully tumultuous experience, but it is hard to keep your impressions under control or to remember what exactly you have seen and what places you have visited.

Your second trip to Venice is different, and perhaps the best one you make in your life, in terms of personal growth, anyway. There is still the freshness and wonder, but with it a new-found sense of familiarity, almost of ownership. You find yourself saying, this is the place where we had drinks last time, so we'll do it again; let's go back to that tiny chapel with the wonderful Carpaccios, and let's do that lovely walk again along the Zattere. But there is still the sense of discovery: I knew it was great, but I didn't know it was *this* great. Amid the familiarity you find many more new things, and with them, the underlying feeling that the place has more in it than you will ever be able to absorb: that this is a place of almost limitless possibilities.

The second spring of a birdlistener is a bit like this second trip to Venice: the wonder of the new is perfectly mixed with the privilege of growing familiarity. That doesn't mean subsequent trips are less rewarding – whether to Venice or the nation of birdsong – but it is during this second trip that the dual experience of novelty and familiarity is at its most acute. Savour, then, your second spring as a birdlistener, and take joy in the birds both new and familiar. At the end of this most wonderful spring, you will be irrevocably committed. So listen out.

Mistle thrush

Perhaps the best bird of my second spring was the first. I remember hearing the song, high across the Suffolk fields, pelting down from the top of a high stag-headed oak. Blackbird, I said at once, and then paused, in the classic manner of the second-spring birdlistener. No, it's not a bloody blackbird, is it? Listen. Listen well.

And listen I did. And I found that the alleged blackbird's song was too quick, the phrases too short, and the whole thing wasn't really blackbird-like at all. It was a song with a completely different quality: it wasn't lazy, it wasn't relaxed; it wasn't in the least bit *dolce far niente*. It was much wilder than a blackbird's: wild, and in some way aspirational, presumptuous, daring. Perhaps that's because it came so early in the year: because the mistle thrush – and mistle thrush it was all right – is one of the first singers to raise his voice. The song is often described as skirling, which means like bagpipes, which is fine as far as it goes, so long as you don't expect the song to be continuous – and the whole point of bagpipes is to make a continuous sound.

No: these are short, melodious, shouted phrases,

delivered with immense élan: a cry in which he is not only telling his rivals to sod off, but telling winter to sod off as well. Mistle thrushes have the nickname of storm-cocks, because they have a taste for singing in difficult conditions: when you get a burst of sun on the most uncompromising sort of spring day, a mistle thrush is liable to lift his voice in song. Sometimes they will be presumptuous enough to start singing before the year has even turned: before Christmas is not unusual; some have heard mistle thrush singing in November.

Mistle thrushes are birds just waiting for the dam to burst: birds full of testosterone and song, agog for the least excuse to let rip. All the early singers bring a special pleasure to the birdlistener: admiration for their bravery and gratitude for their insistence that better times are on their way. Of all these early singers, the mistle thrush is the loudest, the wildest and the most cheering.

They are birds that like to have a good deal of noise around them. They make a loud and unambiguous alarm call, generally compared to the sound of an old-fashioned football rattle. But perhaps that comparison is out of date: a dry, strident rattle, urgent and emotional and rather aggressive. They will give this sound, or at least, a relatively perfunctory version of it, to defend food resources against other birds. But they will also make it around the nest site and this can produce a dramatic spectacle. They are big, burly thrushes, and completely fearless, and so when a magpie comes lurking around the nest in search of a meal of mistle thrush eggs or chicks, the mistle thrush will go for it without a second thought. Often two of them together, rattling dementedly and dive-bombing the magpie till it has been driven off. It is enough to make you wish for a football rattle of your own, so you can cheer for the plucky underdog, and to shout rude words as the magpie makes his retreat while the mistle thrushes give chase and shout still ruder birdwords at the retreating black tail.

Starling

Astarling sings like all the birds you've already learned, and a good few more besides. He does this on purpose: this is a singer that takes the sounds all around and twists and weaves them into a song that is personal and unique.

I sometimes wonder if the starling is not the most spectacular bird in Britain. His lustrous and iridescent purple feathers are beautiful when caught in a certain light. The winter flocking displays, when a million birds will make shapes in the air for the joy of togetherness, are rightly famous. And the bird is a virtuoso mimic and entertainer: for versatility, there is no one to touch him in this country.

For all the mimicry, a starling still mostly sounds like a starling. A burst of starling song tends to be extended and thoughtful, with plenty of whistles and wheezes and bill-clicks that are very clearly starling. But these will be interspersed with all kinds of imitations: some of them perfunctory fragments, others more elaborate and finished. One of the minor pleasures of becoming a birdlistener is to listen to a starling and work out which birds he has included in his repertoire. A starling sings the place he lives in: he encapsulates, in song, the sonic environment, the soundscape he inhabits. You can say that he does this because he is an artist: you can say that he does this because the bigger the repertoire, the more sexy the singer becomes for female starlings, and the more intimidating to males. Either or both: it's a performance to revel in.

An interesting point is that the starling doesn't imitate the birds themselves. He imitates the sounds he hears. That sounds like a subtle point, but it is not. He will make a noise like a *distant* owl – so it won't sound as if there was not a starling but an owl perched on his song post. It helps to keep that in mind as you try and work out what a starling is imitating.

A starling specialises in mimicking other birds. That's because he is a bird himself. Bird sounds are more meaningful to him than any other kinds of sound: an example, if you like, of avian chauvinism, or perhaps ornithomorphism. But he is perfectly prepared to bring in non-avian sounds when they take his fancy. Wolf whistles are a traditional part of starling vocabulary. Car alarms have become a favourite in recent decades. You used often to hear starlings imitating Trimphones: for younger readers, I should explain that a Trimphone was a modernist telephone brought out in the 1960s, and it warbled rather than rang. Starlings liked the sound and took it on: a real bird imitating a machine that was imitating a bird. This Trimphone call persisted some years after Trimphones had gone extinct, their memory kept alive by starlings, who presumably learned the sound from listening to each other. But I haven't heard a Trimphoning starling for years, so I'd guess the call has died out: to be replaced by new ones from the ever-inventive starling. Modern telephones make all kinds of interesting noises, and starlings will take them on. If ever anyone asks you which bird makes a sound like a telephone, you can answer "starling" with very reasonable confidence.

Starlings that have been introduced to human domestic life will pick up fragments of speech. Pliny taught pet starlings Latin and Greek phrases. Oddly – or perhaps not oddly at all – it seems the more you try and ram a phrase into a starling, the less effect it has: starlings like to make their own minds up about what sounds they find amusing, or useful. It's the artist in them, no doubt. American scientists who did research with starlings reported that the phrases they most often heard – "no" and "here's some lettuce" – were never imitated by starlings. But one bird heard a basketball match on television and took on the chant "defence, defence". Another, rather gratifyingly, used to say "basic research".

Learning curve

No starling was born with the ability to imitate a Trimphone, or for that matter, to say "basic research". You don't need much basic research to work that out. Therefore, the starling acquired it during the course of his life. In other words, he learned it. So a starling – obviously – knows how to learn stuff.

There are some kinds of behaviour – in birds, in humans – that are, or seem to be, instinctive, hardwired, something we are born with. There are other things that we – birds and humans – need to learn. And with many species of bird, it has become clear that song is something that needs to be learned. A bird reared in isolation – a bird that can't hear other birds singing – will frequently prove himself incapable of singing properly.

All at once we are in a terrifying jungle of cutting-edge science. The furious arguments about what is learned and what is innate in birdsong catapult us right into the middle of the nature-nurture debate, and on, into the fascinating suggestion that this entire concept represents a false duality, and that nurture is required to release what is innate, which makes the two things inextricable.

It has been shown, for example, that some isolated birds can still develop a repertoire of songs – but it will only be one third the size of the repertoire of a proper wild bird of the same species. However, in a species in which wild birds have big repertoires, isolated birds will still have larger repertoires than those of isolated birds with small repertoires. Some behaviours seem to be more nature-dependent, while others are more nurture-dependent.

And even young birds brought up in the wild don't get their song right at the first crack of the whip. They don't become mature and instantly rip the skies open with a perfect burst of song appropriate to their species. They need to practise. The syrinx – the birds' voice box – is a complicated instrument, and learning to use it properly is a major challenge. That's why you will sometimes hear a bird singing very quietly, more or less humming to himself. But he is not passing the time of day: he is deadly serious. If he is a young bird, he is learning how to sing: if he is an experienced bird, he is practising, relearning, getting ready. This is called subsong, sometimes confusingly called "recording". It is singing without issuing a challenge, without sending out a come-on. The transition from subsong to full song comes with a great surge of testosterone.

A bird matures, so his song stabilises. A repertoire singer establishes a basic library of sounds: now he can start adding to it as he listens to other birds and kicks about in the world. He will learn what hen-birds really prefer. Birds that like to mimic sounds can increase their range. A blackbird was heard imitating a shepherd's whistle to his dog: when the blackbird was recorded and played back to the dog, the dog obeyed.

The spotted bower-bird in Australia is perhaps the world's champion mimic. A single individual was heard to make the sounds of many other species of bird and to mix in with these imitations the sounds of barking dogs, cattle breaking through scrub, a woodman striking a splitter's wedge and emus crashing through a twanging wire fence.

Birds learn all right. Of course they do: it's a matter of life and death.

Mozart's starling

Mozart heard a starling whistling a fragment of his own Piano Concerto in G major 455. He bought the starling, writing down the details of the purchase in his diary of expenses. He also jotted down the music the bird sang. It was a remarkable performance from the starling because the concerto had not actually been published on the date in question, May 27, 1784. Perhaps the only two people who knew the melody were Mozart and the pupil for whom he had composed the piece. Mozart was a great public whistler and had been to the shop before, so perhaps the starling heard Mozart, liked the tune and annexed it for his own repertoire. Or perhaps it was the pupil.

Mozart noted that the starling had not only learned the bit of Mozart music: he had also adapted it. "G natural was changed to a G sharp, immediately making the tune sound centuries ahead of its time," wrote the musician and birdsong enthusiast David Rothenberg.

The bird died three years later, and Mozart held a funeral for him, with guests decked out in mourning. Mozart read some lines of his own:

A little fool lies here
Whom I held dear –
A starling in the prime
Of his brief time …

The event has not gone down well in history. It was the week Mozart's father died, for a start. Some like to put this down as an example of his immaturity and his taste for silliness. But perhaps this is a failure of the imagination. Perhaps Mozart liked the starling for something more than sentimentality. Perhaps he admired the starling as a fellow musician; perhaps he genuinely, rather then facetiously or ironically, loved the starling for his – innate, but also learned – virtuosity and creativity. And perhaps something about the starling's tendency to long, free-flowing, somewhat unstructured verses appealed to Mozart as an alternative way of organising material.

Rothenberg claims that Mozart's chamber piece K522, "A Musical Joke", was inspired by the starling. "After hearing a starling who learned one of his own melodies, Mozart wrote a piece where he learned from the disjointed, rather unclassical, and certainly non-human musical sense that marks the starling's song." He then quotes, by means of musical notation, the cadenza to the andante cantabile movement, and declares that this is nothing more nor less than the song of a starling. This is not just Mozart imitating a starling in the course of a piece of effortless virtuosity: here a starling is permitted to dictate not just the sound but the actual structure of the piece. The starling was co-composer: deserving equal billing with Wolfgang Amadeus Mozart.

Goldcrest

Only a birdlistener hears a goldcrest. This, then, is something of a watershed bird: when you have got this one sorted out, you know you've passed some kind of test. It's not a terribly hard one: the song is unmistakable and the bird is widespread and easily found. It's just that the nature of the song makes it something the non-birdlistener automatically tunes out. It's not that people ignore it: they don't even hear it. You need to make a small but crucial mental adjustment if you are to hear goldcrests. You have to have developed the habit of listening out for birds. You need to be a birdlistener.

Once you have done that, you will hear plenty of goldcrests. Tiny things, busy high up in trees, not fond of bird tables: they are not straightforward birds to see. For that reason, they are not part of our shared awareness, as robins are. The song takes a little bit of listening to, because it's so high – so much so that with increasing age, birders often lose the bird altogether. Higher frequencies are the first ones to go with age, and the high, thin little song of the goldcrest is the first one the ageing birder starts to miss.

Goldcrests sing early in the spring, especially on nice

days. They are liable to occasional bursts of song for much of the year. Listen out at the foot of trees, especially conifers; stretch your ears for this falsetto warble, this high, rapid, rhythmic tumbling of notes. It sounds more or less exactly as you would expect the smallest bird in Britain to sound.

The song comes in brief bursts of a couple of seconds, a slithering run with a bit of a flourish at the end. There'll usually be another offering soon afterwards. It always sounds pretty much the same: this is a singer who believes in stereotypical rather than inventive song, though I have read that the flourished endings of the song are highly individual. Sometimes, at exciting moments, the bird will extend a song for a good deal longer and throw in as many individual flourishes as possible.

This is a bird that likes to sing. In spring they go in for leisurely song-duels with nearby rivals, in a manner that seems not so much a state of chronic opposition as a search for security, each bird safe in his own abutting territory. The goldcrest calls have the same quality as their song: quite tremendously high and thin. The goldcrest song reminds me of those slightly feeble fireworks that emit a rain of golden sparks and, er, that's it. They are nothing compared with the noisy detonations of more spectacular singers: but an essential part of any box of fireworks.

Green woodpecker

In spring you are likely to hear outbursts of maniacal laughter: great loud explosions of hilarity. It's an appropriate sound for the time of year: as if sex-crazed creatures from deep mythology were crashing about through the bushes in search of fun – and finding it, too, from the sound of it.

The laughers are green woodpeckers, making the sound that gives them the excellent nickname of yaffle. They don't go in for much drumming; they will do it occasionally, but it's not what they're best at, and the sound is a little apologetic after the forthright Ginger-Bakering of the great spotted woodpecker. Green woodpeckers are better when they laugh.

It's a very variable laugh, with any number of ha-has and ho-hos in it: from one to maybe 30. It fades away a little towards the close, falling a little in pitch as it does so. It's a bit like a high-pitched version of the laughter you hear when the terrified man, fleeing the fearful fiend, crashes panic-stricken into his room, locks the doors and the window and draws the curtain, only to hear the voice say: "Now we're locked in together." Cue the maniacal laugh.

The different kinds and different lengths of laughter serve different functions: the longest calls come when they are calling attention to themselves, in display; the shorter ones are for alarm and other kinds of excitement. At these times they will usually favour a three-syllable laugh.

You will often hear this laughter in open country, low to the ground, which may seem odd, since this bird is supposed to be a woodpecker. But green woodpeckers are great eaters of ants, and love to get down on the ground and use their woodpecking beaks to demolish ants' nests. When alarmed, or when interacting with each other in an exuberant way, they will break into bursts of laughter. You will often see them flying away from you in open country: switchbacking in classic woodpecker fashion, the green bodies picked out with bright yellow bums that flash the alarm to other birds. Richard Mabey, that excellent nature-writer, once wrote that green woodpeckers in flight look like little dragons, a comparison so stupendously apt that I think of it almost every time I see a green woodpecker fly by.

They are noisy birds, and in the autumn, the young birds kick up a fair amount of din. Hear the laughter: turn your eyes to the retreating laugher, and you will find your dragon.

Portrait of the artist

I said something about the starling being an artist. Was I making a musical joke? Was I being face-tious? Was I using the term as a kind of literary flourish, trying to express something of the bird's nature without wishing to be taken literally? Did I mean that the bird is *like* an artist? Or did I mean that the bird is a genuinely creative being, one that is deliberately seeking to express himself and his environment? One that is deliberately making music?

I am not a hundred per cent certain of the answer to any of those questions. I don't suppose a starling is likely to be interviewed on a late-night arts programme: "What I am seeking to do with my music is encapsulate the sound that my landscape makes. Being a bird myself, I naturally include many sounds of birds, but I also feel that by bringing in other sounds, including those that you humans make, we can reach some kind of trans-specific understanding. And that's what my art is really all about: to reach out beyond the boundaries not only of species but of genus and family and order and even class. As a performer and composer, I see my task as an attempt to reach other kinds of vertebrates – vertebrates like yourselves, mammals, humans – and by doing so, to reinforce the essential truth of life: that we are all of us alive on this planet and subject to its laws."

David Rothenberg was looking a little battered when he came to my place. Rothenberg, who wrote about Mozart's starling in *Why Birds Sing*, was making a television programme with the same title. He is a jazz clarinettist, and he has often played his clarinet to birds in the National Aviary in Pittsburgh. The birds responded. And so, being a musician himself, he responded to the way the birds responded to him. They adjusted their song for him: he adjusted the music he was playing for them, and so between them they created music across species, and across the classes of Aves and Mammalia.

Check him out. You can listen to the music on www.whybirdssing.com. It's fascinating stuff. As a musician first and a philosopher second, Rothenberg is convinced that birds like music for its own sake. He doesn't think that musicianship is something that can be explained by biological function alone. His key point is that birdsong is more beautiful than it needs to be. More complex, more moving than would be necessary if birdsong were nothing more than a biological signalling process. Bleep-bleep: this is my place. Bleep-bleep-bleep: I'm ready for a female. Bleep-bleep-bleep-bleep: I'm a hell of a guy.

But instead we have the skylark that pours and pelts music, till none's to spill or spend.

Rothenberg was battered because had been talking

to scientists, and they had absolutely no idea what he was talking about. Scientists are invariably the first to admit ignorance in their own field: a scientist, of all kinds of expert, will always be the first to say: "I just don't know." Scientists are not the arrogant people they are sometimes supposed to be. But science is also a way of thinking, a world-view that can make it difficult to accommodate other world-views. The ornithologists Rothenberg talked to simply didn't get him. They saw the whole business that had engaged him so profoundly as something irrelevant to their own cutting-edge researches on such things as learned and innate behaviour. The question of whether or not a starling was an artist had never occurred to them: it was not the way their minds worked. For them the question had no meaning. And they were, alas, narrow enough to feel that Rothenberg was not just following a different road, but just plain wrong.

They made no effort to adjust to Rothenberg's thinking. This was disappointing to anybody who thought that these scientists might turn out to be polymaths. So Rothenberg and I set out chairs in a copse behind my house, with the cameras up in front, and an increasingly exasperated director behind the camera. The problem was that Rothenberg hadn't been out in the field with anyone who knew British birdsong, so every time a bird sang – in other words, every few seconds – I told him what it was, and he listened and we discussed it. We got the telly stuff done eventually, and then we stayed exactly where we were while the crew packed up. Listening to birds, talking about birdmusic and humanmusic.

I am not a scientist. I have done my share of reading around zoological subjects, but I haven't been trained to think in that very direct way that research scientists must cultivate. So I had no problem at all with the idea that the song thrush, who was firing out careless raptures for us from the summit of an oak 50 yards away, was taking some kind of pleasure in his performance. A song thrush is a repertoire singer: putting together an individual repertoire is by definition a creative act. I don't suppose the thrush put the repertoire together by thinking only of sex and territory: the sounds themselves must have their appeal. If we are going to be reductionist about this, then the simplest way of understanding the song of the thrush is to accept that the thrush is getting a bang from the music itself.

Birdsong is an aspect of biological destiny. It's not a sideline. For a male songbird, music is not optional: it is not optional for a female either, for that matter. But I wonder: does a female hear a bravura performance from a male song thrush and think solely about making eggs? Or does the music itself touch her?

Obviously, science is not going to provide the answer to this sort of questioning any time soon – though there has been evidence to suggest that the song of the male nightingale makes chemical changes to the brain of the female. The fact is that this sort of questioning about bird-as-artist gets complicated very fast, and mostly because we keep thinking of humans as completely separate life forms from anything else on the planet. It is, after all, the way we have been trained to think across the millennia.

But certainly, as we have already established, it's a fact that we humans not only have biological urges, we also take pleasure in fulfilling them. Are we really alone in creation in this? We fill television with celebrations of these biological pleasures. Cooking programmes are about the way we gratify our urge to eat and therefore survive. Humans are not alone in thinking one kind of nutritious food is more palatable than another kind, as anyone who has kept a domestic animal knows. Most of the films we watch are about biological urges: the urge to find and keep a mate is at the base of rom-coms, the urge to acquire or defend a territory and/or status is at the back of most thrillers. *Romeo and Juliet* and *Macbeth* are both plays about biological urges and how we cope with them: that doesn't stop them being the finest kind of art.

The question of whether birds are conscious musicians or whether they are "merely" responding to biological urges seems to be a non-question. They make music: and only musicians make music. The question of whether or not they *see* it as music is not a question about music but about philosophy: and I am not prepared to make a case for birds as philosophers; not today, anyway.

But birds make music, and it is all around us. The best singers – in bird terms – get the best mates and the best territories. Therefore it pays to make the best music you can. The life of a male songbird is all about becoming the best singer he can possibly be. Song is more important to a bird than it is to any human: perhaps there is a case for saying that for that reason, birds are more committed artists than any human could ever be.

Birdsong gives me pleasure: I suspect both singing and listening to birdsong give birds pleasure. But the idea of pleasure is complex, so let's close this chapter on a note of certainty. For a songbird, singing is fulfilment.

Goldfinch

Goldfinches were almost loved to death. The combination of a spectacular appearance and a deeply pleasing song was irresistible: they were trapped in thousands, some to become cage birds and some to be stuffed as tasteful ornaments. When the Society for the Protection of Birds – later the RSPB – was formed in the late 19th century, they saw one of their first tasks as saving the goldfinches. In this, as with many other species and places and other conservation matters, they did a fine job. (And if you are now a birdlistener and not yet a member of the RSPB, please amend this anomaly immediately.)

Goldfinches light up our countryside: the brightness of their sound and their appearance are equally dazzling. They are a fine contradiction to the rule that says good singers tend to have drab plumage. Their collective noun is a favourite with everybody: a charm of goldfinches. And it's a term that works equally well with the dazzling black-and-yellow flashing of their wings as they pass, or the bouncing, tinkling calls they exchange between them as they do so.

You are likely to hear goldfinches throughout the

year, but in spring, as you'd expect, they make a special effort. The song is a great rush of jangling and tinkling notes – golden notes, it always seems to me, as if the sound were being played on tiny instruments of gold. There is a reckless, and, in a quiet way, a slightly over-whelming quality about a goldfinch in full song: it is as if he has to get a certain number of notes out before a rather right deadline. The hurry detracts from the musical quality a little, but as it is part of the bird's essential charm, this doesn't seem too much of a draw-back. The song tends to be full of sharp buzzy elem-ents: these are the things to listen out for as you are learning. The goldfinch buzz is much harsher than the zweee of a greenfinch, and besides, the greenfinch's song is far more relaxed.

Goldfinches are usually seen in small flocks in the winter, and they will call to each other, on the ground, in trees, and especially in flight. The call tends to be a bright and cheerful three syllables, the middle one more or less swallowed.

Once you have picked out your goldfinch with the aid of the buzzing, you should listen to the song, not only for its cheeriness and beauty, but in order to familiarise yourself with its essential quality. This is not a bad technique with all the birds you listen to, but it is particularly relevant for the goldfinch. Once you have absorbed the way the bird sings, you will start to pick up the full range of goldfinch sounds. This, by the way, will give you a fine trick to impress your friends. Tell them that you can hear a willow warbler, and they will say "Oh yes?" and change the subject. But if you can hear a goldfinch and then point out a bunch of the little stunners, people will suddenly realise what you are on about. Produce a goldfinch for them on call – like a rabbit from a hat – and people will suddenly realise that you are a genius, and that they have underestimated you all these years.

Yellowhammer

The yellowhammer's song has the most famous mnemonic of them all: and it is seriously misleading. "A little bit of bread and no cheese." It seems to me that the mnemonic has gathered its own impetus somehow and overshadowed the actual song. It's a bit more like "bread-bread-bread-bread-bread-bread*chee-eeese*". Except that sometimes the bird doesn't bother with the cheese.

But it's a good bird to listen out for, often on open farm landscape with good hedges to lurk about in and low trees to sing from, though the bird will happily sing from a wire. The bread part of the song rises briefly in intensity, a succession of gently accelerating sweet notes. The optional cheese part of the song is more of a whistle, often in two elided syllables.

Yellowhammers start to sing with the first bright weather of the year: but they don't give up. They carry on into the early summer, when most of the birds around them have given up, so if you haven't got them in the rising chorus of the spring, don't give up. Keep listening, and you will be probably be able to work him out before the summer ends.

The rhythmician

Mozart's starling did his stint as a composer, but that was largely the result of Mozart's highly developed – if not always terribly subtle – sense of humour. But Olivier Messiaen went the whole way. For him, there was no joke involved, none at all. He didn't think it was amusing that birds could create something that sounded like human music: he thought it was a vitally important fact of life that birds brought music into human life, and he celebrated it in a series of extraordinary compositions.

He liked to say that he was a better ornithologist than any other composer, and a better musician than any other ornithologist. He described himself as an ornithologist and rhythmician. He wrote a vast seven-volume work, *Traité de rhythme, de couleur et d'ornithologie*, containing many field transcriptions of birdsong into musical notation.

But above all, he gave us the *Catalogue d'oiseaux*. "At times of unhappiness, when my uselessness has become brutally apparent to me and all musical language seems to be reduced to the result of patient experiment without anything behind the notes justifying all the effort – what then can one do but seek one's true, forgotten face somewhere in the forest, the meadows, in the mountains, on the beach – in the midst of the birds ... the birds are the real artists – they are the true originators of my pieces."

The *Catalogue* brings us more than three hours of music, played on a solo piano. If they were no more than evocations of landscape, they would be wonderful enough: translating the sight of mountains and forests into sound, confusing the senses in the manner of an acid-trip, a process known as synaesthesia.

But from these sonic landscapes the birds raise their voices in song. To those who know birdsong, they are astonishing; accurate and utterly recognisable, but never slavish, just as the imitations given by song thrush and blackbird and starling are not slavish. This piece, first performed in 1958, is one of my iPod favourites: complex and uplifting, the more so because it makes the world beyond humanity so vivid and accessible. "I give birdsongs to those who dwell in cities and have never heard them." And even those who know birdsongs well will hear them as if for the first time when they listen to the formidable mysteries of the *Catalogue*.

Messiaen first began to write birdmusic – or collaborate with birds, as perhaps he would prefer – when he was a prisoner of war in Verdun in 1940. In the *Catalogue* he takes that most civilised of all instruments, the piano, that great unwieldy thing that you find in drawing rooms and concert halls, and turns it wild, creating mountains and forests and rivers and peopling them with choughs and warblers and owls and thrushes and larks.

He was once asked if he thought that nature did things better than civilisation. "I dare not answer – my response would be that civilisation has spoiled us, has taken away our freshness of observation."

I have written this book in the hope that those who read it may become a little less civilised: that something of that freshness of observation can be found again. And as both celebration and as learning aid, I suggest you try the *Catalogue*.

Nuthatch

If you live in an area with plenty of mature trees, you might have another of those pleasant surprises that coms with a growing knowledge of birdsong. Nuthatches are much commoner than you thought. They are great visitors to bird tables, where they are the most resolutely inverted of all birds, neat and natty with too much kohl around the eyes, and easily distinguishable because their heads are at the bottom and their tails at the top.

They are very vocal and highly distinctive. They are probably the best whistlers we have. They use a trilling referee's whistle and a strong, clear, untrilled whistle, and they mix and match them at will. They are strongly territorial, and will often call during the winter. As spring starts to arrive, they shift into song, and loud and clear is the way they like to do it.

The sound carries a considerable distance, and, as is usual in forest birds, it cuts through the ambient noise and the muffled acoustic of a foliage-filled canopy. Rainforest birding is notable for strong and marvellously clear sounds emerging from vegetation no binoculars could ever penetrate. The nuthatch, mostly high in the canopy and well out of sight, does its best to translate that tradition into the woods of Britain. They are also at home in the suburbs, wherever we have kept enough big trees, and they are often to be found in parks and commons, so long as the country isn't too open. Hear an arboreal referee signalling another terrible foul from way above your head, and you have found your nuthatch.

Coal tit

You have worked out the great tit, and then sorted out the blue tit. But there is a third common garden tit, another indefatigable visitor to bird-feeders, and you need to get him clear in your mind. You have probably already had the experience of listening to a bird, knowing that it is a tit, but not being quite sure whether it is blue or great: not bossy enough for great tit, but not quite right for blue tit.

This is your coal tit: the tiniest of the common tits, black head with a little white splash at the back, giving the bird a slightly badger-like appearance. The great tit, as we know, says teacher-teacher. Perhaps it is helpful to say that the great tit goes teacher-teacher while the coal tit goes teacherteacherteacherteacher.

The coal tit sounds exactly like a speeded-up great tit: the song is both faster and higher, much as you'd expect from so little a bird. Being a tit, they have all sorts of variations and complications. Like all tits, they make a few simple sounds go an awfully long way. But tits as a family are pretty distinctive, so that gives you a straight-forward starting place. When you come down to the which-tit phase, then it is helpful enough to remember the size. The great tit is great, and therefore the loudest and most strident; the blue tit comes in the middle and is therefore the middlest as well as the bluest; and the coal tit is tiny and therefore tends to be higher and faster than the other two.

And if you find this even slightly confusing, then remember to rejoice that we have so many tits to revel in. Being confused is just one more way of revelling in biodiversity: you wouldn't have known there were so many different kinds of bird if you hadn't taken the trouble to get confused.

a. Great Tit
b. Blue Tit
c. Coal Tit

Rhythm section

If you spend time with Bill Oddie you hear an awful lot of humming. Music matters to him: music is rarely out of his thoughts or off his lips. As the two of us travelled round Zambia, doing a trip on behalf of a the World Land Trust – I am a council member, Bill a long-time supporter – there was an awful lot of tumtumming and pompomming going on.

"Listen to the rhythm!" Bill said that on more than one occasion, for time and again, it was the rhythm – rather than the melody – of the natural sounds that moved him. The frogs that tinkled in their Chinese windchime chorus; the white fronted bee-eaters that called to each other in flight, the calls of the long-tailed glossy starlings as they foraged on the ground, the crickets that called at night: all of them had a rhythm, and whether or not it was intended, it was part of the pattern of life out in the bush.

That hard, unbroken, 4/4 rhythm that is behind most rock music, the heartbeat rhythm to which every mammal begins the process of life: that's one thing. But there is rhythm of a more elusive kind in the other sounds of the natural world. After all, Messiaen called himself a rhythmician, and perhaps rhythmic complexity is the single most remarkable thing about the *Catalogue*.

Birds are musicians, and all music has a rhythm of some kind, however irregular, disjointed and hard to follow. Sometimes the rhythm is part of the structure of a bird's song – something you will hear most obviously with the repetitions of song thrush. There is a rhythm, though a far less obvious one, to the unending unbroken song of skylarks.

But sometimes the rhythm is apparently driven by chance. In the chirping of sparrows around the rooftops, in the quacking of a flock of fieldfare, in the screaming of black-headed gulls around a rubbish dump, you can hear the suggestion of rhythm, one that you no sooner begin to tap your foot to than it shifts, changes, fades, speeds up. Are the birds themselves aware of it? Do they respond to the elusive rhythm of the sounds they make together?

Certainly, rhythm is a helpful concept to us, as we strive to understand and hear and learn birdsong, not least because as mammals we have a deep taste for it. What it means to birds, still less to frogs and crickets, I can't say with any certainty. But all creatures who make deliberate sounds respond to sounds: otherwise there would be no point in making them. A response that is in a loose – and often enough in a tight – sense rhythmical seems to me to be a natural way of relating to a fellow creature, especially one of the same species. And I think the idea of rhythm is, cautiously, a pretty helpful way to help humans listen to birds.

I remember what was perhaps Bill's finest moment as a wildlife presenter. He was listening to corncrakes, one of those birds that can say their own scientific name: *Crex crex*. And he started to hum *The Blue Danube*:

> Da dada da dum –
> And the bird cut in: Crex crex! Crex crex!
> Da dada da *dum* –
> Crex crex! Crex crex!
> Rhythm of life.

Pied wagtail

The call is something you hear all the time, and it is important to get it straight in your mind, not only for its own sake, but so that you can be quite sure it's not anything else. I often hear pied wagtails on the banks of the Thames when I am in London; I generally stay in Mortlake, near the finish of the Boat Race. The crews stop racing just before Chiswick Bridge, and then drift through its centre arch in agonised triumph or still more agonised despair.

Chiswick! That's precisely the call of the pied wagtail. I have seen one fly over Chiswick Bridge loudly calling the name of the bridge as he did so. (I don't think Chiswick breaks the pee-ooo rule, does it?)

Pied wagtails call frequently, often because they like to be in touch with the other half of a pair. They like to call in flight, often when they take off and come in to land. It's a bright and cheerful two syllables, as buoyant as the bird's bouncing flight. They don't have anything that you can really call a song, but they will bundle together a few variants around the Chiswick theme. Once you've got that essential call, the rest of the bird's repertoire is pretty easy to pick out. They are jolly, sparky little birds, and their simple repertoire adds to the gaiety of the world.

Meadow pipit

Pay attention. This is one of those rather dull, basic lessons you'll thank me for later, especially if you concentrate. And there's a rather fabulous bonus at the end of it. But first, you must learn your meadow pipit call, because if you can't, you will always be confused when you are in open and upland areas.

You will hear meadow pipits all the time, and it is essential to sort them out because if you don't, you won't be able to pick out anything else. Meadow pipits are the ambient birds of these places, and most of the small brown birds you see and hear will be meadow pipits. But not all: so you need to get the call and the song of meadow pipits logged, because that's the only way you will be able to pick out birds that are not meadow pipits.

They are not great vocalists. They sound like little brown jobs, as well as look like them. Their basic call is to say their own name, pipit, though often enough they will just give you a pip. They will give a higher call in alarm, often on the wing, flying away from you: that's probably the most important call to learn.

The song is pretty ordinary, not much melody to it,

though they are pretty keen on rhythm, giving a series of cheeping notes. But – and here is the bonus – every now and then in spring they will go into a song flight. The cheeping will double in passion and commitment, the bird will rise into the air, making a huge fuss of itself, and then parachute down to earth like a giant shuttlecock.

It's an extraordinary piece of drama from one of our least dramatic-looking birds. It seems total insanity for a bird that would make a very handy meal for any passing bird of prey: it's as if the bird is deliberately taunting all the sparrowhawks of the region. It is this detonation of sound and extravagance and sheer recklessness that is needed to win a hen pipit's heart, and to convince a rival male that here is a pipit that's not to be messed with.

All birds are spectacular. Even – or perhaps especially – the drabbest. In appearance and song, meadow pipits are the pinnacle of dullness: and yet they have within them one of the spectacular moments of the birding year.

Peasant and phartridge

Peasants and phartridges, James Joyce called them, and so do I. Still, better get their sounds clear in your head, because they're all over the place, and if you don't have them sorted, you'll get led astray every time you take a walk in the country, and that would never do. After all, the shooting people release 40 million pheasants into the countryside every year, so you're going to hear a good few of them. Never in the history of life has any species faired so well because it is so good at dying.

Cock pheasants crow. They do it throughout the year, but naturally, they double their efforts in spring. At this time, they will often find themselves a small eminence and there they will follow the crow with a violent whirring of the wings. It is the most preposterously conceited bit of bird behaviour you will ever come across: if Mr Toad were a bird, he'd disport himself like a cock pheasant. Pheasants are also the least cool birds. They try to adopt the strategy of concealment, but they simply haven't got the nerve for it. At the last moment, they will take to the air – always a hard thing for a pheasant to do, which is what makes them such amusing targets – uttering a series of mad clucking and crowing noises, often leaving behind them a walker who has jumped three feet in the air, or a horse that has spooked sideways.

The native grey partridge is a very unusual bird these days, alas, so the shooting people have stocked the countryside with the alien red-legged partridge. They are often heard in and around open fields, often towards the edges, by the hedge. They make a series of croaky, clucky, rhythmic sounds. There is a closely related bird called a chukar, also released into this country, and the red-legged partridges will often express themselves in a series of chukar-chukar-chukars.

Now let's get back to the real birds.

Be happy!

It's that moment in the second spring of the bird-listener when it suddenly all makes sense. In a single second, you will realise why you went to the trouble of reading this book. And that reason is joy.

The moment of joy will come to you when you hear the first migrant of your second spring: and it will continue as the other migrants come in. You will be filled with joy because you recognise some of the birds, and because you will be aware that some are new and you will start to learn them. There will be joy in the beauty of the songs and double and triple joy in the coming of the spring.

The Greeks have a fine greeting: *herete*! It is an imperative; it's nothing less than an order: be happy! In *My Family and Other Animals*, Gerald Durrell, in the chapter called "The Sweet Spring", responds to an exchange of this greeting: "Be happy. How could one be anything else in such a season?"

There are many good reasons for becoming a birdlistener. It helps you tell one bird from another; it helps you build a list of birds; it adds interest to a nice walk, it is essential for making an ornithological survey; it tells you about music; it tells you about melody and rhythm; it tells you about biodiversity; it asks the most fascinating questions about learned and innate behaviour. I have written this book with all those noble and important reasons in mind, but the greatest of all reasons for listening to birds is that each and every bird is capable of making the listener happy: for an instant, for a day, for a season, for a lifetime.

So you will listen to the chiffchaff, the first warbler to return to our shores, and as they utter their strongly rhythmic chant, mostly from the tops of high trees, you will greet them as old friends, as the first birds that return to us for the great season of happiness.

Soon enough you will be picking up the other migrants as they fly in: the merry and complex twittering of the swallow, the mixture of rich notes and harsh grating ones from the blackcap, and the sweet slithering-down-the-scale from the willow warbler. The great drama of the spring centres around the migrants, and you will find yourself involved in it as never before.

And still with more to learn. As happy a thought as you could wish for. *Herete*!

House martin

House martins make farting noises. Or aerial rasp-berries, if you prefer. They fly in, more or less with the swallows, and make their mud nests under the over-hanging eaves of houses. Sad to say, they do so in smaller numbers than they did before, but they are still seen often enough: easily distinguishable from swallows as they belly-skim the grass because of their white bums.

And because of the sound they make. They are birds that are only truly happy when there are quite a lot of them, and they keep in contact with each other by means of these brief trilled raspberries. Tune into that really quite unmistakable sound, and when you hear it above your head, you know you will look up and see a merry party of martins, generally hawking for insects.

They also have a song, and a pretty little twittering thing it is too, but it's rather quiet, and it's not terribly relevant for identification. They only sing very close to – and actually from – the nest: they like to nest in colonies, and so they are never defending a territory in any megalomaniacal sense of the term. All they need to protect is the actual nest (and the female within it) so it's only the neighbours who need to hear it. If you are

inside a house with martins, you can often hear the song from the upstairs rooms, but it will usually be inaudible from the ground below.

These birds see themselves as part of a flock even during the breeding season, the most intensely individual time of the year. That's why their most characteristic sound is one of solidarity rather than opposition: the cheerful aerial farting.

Garden warbler

The longest piece in Messiaen's *Catalogue d'oiseaux* is *La Fauvette des jardins*: the garden warbler. On my recording it lasts for 33 minutes 24 seconds. A bit of a special one, then. But also, something of a connoisseur's bird. A bird to learn and grow used to: a bird that you will only just begin to get the hang of in your second spring as a birdlistener.

Garden warblers are famously confusable with blackcaps. I have a sure-fire way of never being wrong about the two species: never look. Always take your own word for it. But if you listen to both birds in full song, you'll find that they really aren't all that much like each other. That stands to reason: when a bird sings, it needs its song to be instantly understood by its own species. As we have seen, birds have finer aural perception than us humans, but it is against the bird's interest to have any hint of confusion in the message it is sending out. Ambiguity is never on the agenda when it comes to song. The blackcap has more of those harsh and challenging notes, and all of those really rich, extravagant fluting notes. The blackcap also has a great deal more structure: versi-fication: stop and start.

But never mind what the garden warbler isn't: let's get on to what the garden warbler actually is. It really does warble: more than any other species of warbler, in the sense of giving out of lot of pretty and fairly rapid musical notes. It's song is not as continuous as the skylark's – nothing is – but it likes comparatively lengthy phrases. The song has a rambling, rather exploratory feel about it: as if the bird were improvising and was never quite sure where the musical idea was going to go: but somehow rescuing the whole thing from confusion by means of its own subtle virtuosity.

The song lacks hard stresses and strong pure notes: it has an almost conversational feel, even in pace and tone, not seeking to shock and startle, but to make a rather elaborate, though unemphatic personal statement. You'll hear them singing from cover. Often around head-height and just above: thoughtful, controlled, quietly inventive, full of personal variations and elusive imitations. They are birds to wait for: to let the song unfold in its carefully woven, non-strident way. The garden warbler is a self-effacing maestro: a virtuoso of understatement. They like to sing, and will carry on quite late in the season. And as I have said, they will carry on singing once they reach their wintering grounds in southern Africa: a sudden extrusion of the English spring into Africa: into the wooded savannahs where the garden warblers forget about gardens and sing instead to the elephants.

Whitethroat

A whitethroat's song is generally described as scratchy. Or sometimes as graty, or grating. There's always a bit of a croak in the song, a hint of Rod Stewart. A friend of mine who ran a pub rock band was always telling the female singer: "Sing dirty!" Get that touch of a growl and a roar and a crack into the voice: rock music is supposed to be simple, but God help it if it's ever pure.

The whitethroat is the Rod Stewart of the warblers, the warbler that likes to sing dirty. You'll hear them from hedges: they like the thick vegetation and dense cover of a hedge. The moment when a hedge I had planted at my place had grown thick enough to house a white-throat was one to be treasured.

They will sing a short phrase of scratchy song from cover at pretty regular intervals. They also like dense bramble thickets. Their call is recognisably of the same quality as their song, but a little more breathy, even wheezy, and noticeably rhythmical.

Every now and then, the singing whitethroat will appear to take leave of his senses: to suffer from an acute attack of ecstasy. His song will suddenly become more intense and a great deal sweeter, and he will rise from his hedge in a glorious moment of fulfilment, flaunting and curvetting in the air above his place of concealment: hang the sparrowhawks, I'm fabulous and I don't care who knows it. The same elevated and enhanced song can sometimes be heard as the whitethroat travels from one song post to another across his territory, or when things are at their most intense with a hen-bird.

Whitethroats are still common enough in agricultural land, wherever there are decent hedges. They are briefly ubiquitous: and then the spring ends and they fall silent and are gone.

Nightingale

A nd finally, to the champion. The nightingale, the singer of singers. This is the one bird in the book that you won't come across by chance. Unlikely, anyway. For a nightingale, most of us must make a pilgrimage. If you don't have birding friends to tell you where to find a nightingale, then ring up your local RSPB office, or your local county Wildlife Trust. You should, of course, also make sure you join these important organisations, otherwise you'd feel terribly guilty and that would compromise your pleasure.

Nightingales are only just British birds. They are on the edge of their range here, and you only find them in the south of the country. If you live in the north, that makes for a quite a long pilgrimage – say, to the RSPB's famous Minsmere reserve – but trust me: it's not something you're going to regret.

Nightingales sing at night. But they also sing during the day. For a brief few weeks – from late April to the beginning of June – they sing almost without cessation. And then the show's over. They shut up for a year, till they next come to their breeding grounds. Even in the daylight cacophony of the high spring, nightingales stand out from the rest. But in the night, they are quite astonishing. I have arrived at Minsmere at three in the morning, stepped from the car, and before taking a step, I have been deafened with the most passionate burst of nightingale song from just behind the reserve offices. In the background, the great basso thump of the bittern – but that's Minsmere for you.

Elsewhere, in pursuit of nightingales, I have stepped from another car and heard nothing. "Really, there was a nightingale singing here last night." "Well, he's not now." We returned the following night – to hear the air filled with song. We walked a mile before we got close, so far does this quite amazing song carry on a still night.

It is a song of endless complexity: in one study, a male demonstrated 250 different phrases put together from a repertoire of 600 different basic sound units. There are two basic and unmistakable bits of nightingale song: the first, an unbelievably clear and passionate whistling, short notes that gather in intensity and volume till the song gains an orgasmic intensity, like the deli scene in *When Harry Met Sally*. The second part is a deep throbbing drumming. The nightingale is not all about such straightforward concepts as beauty: passion and volume that are his forte.

Twit twit twit
Jug jug jug jug jug jug

As T.S. Eliot wrote in *The Waste Land*, a rare example of the great poet breaking the pee-oo rule.

But the nightingale will not only give us melody and rhythm: he will also throw in a great number of equally astonishing harsh and even coarse phrases: croaking and grating, before switching effortlessly into the purest notes imaginable. The range is astonishing: the song itself is utterly overwhelming. A recording – one in which you have control over the volume switch – gives only the merest hint of the experience of hearing a nightingale for real. Once you have heard the song, it is utterly unmistakable, something that, with very little practice, you will be able to recognise almost before the first note is completed. The bird really is that much of an individual, that much of a stand-out.

There is so much effort, so much anxiety, so much triumph, so much joy, and above all, so much music in the song of the nightingale that it is impossible to believe that the nightingale is blindly responding, like a clock, to the working of some interior mechanism. It is impossible to listen to a nightingale without getting the impression that you are listening to a creature that loves song for its own sake, for whom the sound itself is a matter of central and life-affirming purpose. The bird has an answer to Descartes, should he wish to repeat his notion that no non-human creature has a real existence, because it can't think as he did. To Descartes, the night-ingale responds: *canto ergo sum*.

If you were ever tempted by the idea that a non-human creature could be a conscious artist, the nightingale will tip you over the edge. To deny the nightingale an acknowledgment of his intentional and even conscious brilliance seems to me an act of perversity. Some philosophers would argue otherwise, but then some phil-osophers have never sat beneath a nightingale tree on a warm May night.

Some listeners have praised the nightingale's pauses almost as much as the song itself: the way the bird seems artfully to create moments of suspense and promise and then, by exquisite delay, to fulfil them a hundredfold. The nightingale has been written about and praised and has inspired poets again and again: but the remarkable thing is that the bird itself is never a let-down. It is as astonishing to me every May as it was when I first isolated the song more than 20 years ago.

Some listeners have found the song too much. *Birds Britannica*, that spectacular reference book, quotes Lord Edward Grey, statesman and ornithologist, saying that he would never swap blackbirds for nightingales: "It's a song to listen to, but not to live with." The book also quotes Louis Halle, an American naturalist: "It is the same with Bach. With Botticelli. Or with Shakespeare. Sometimes one prays the song will stop."

Certainly, the shatteringly over-the-top nature of the nightingale's song is the most obvious thing about it. Geoff Sample, in his excellent *Bird Songs & Calls*, says that the nightingale's is "more the song of a vocal athlete than a skilled musician. It blasts rather like an operatic diva or a lead guitar in a heavy metal band."

Me, I'm inclined to put that response down to the strange specialisation that comes from truly intense study, as ageing football writers profess that they find more pleasure in a local non-league match than in the World Cup final. But it is important to understand the completely overwhelming quality of the nightingale: the fact that the song affects humans with an almost unique intensity. Lord knows what it does to female nightingales.

Heartache

As every old master had to paint a Virgin Mary, so it seems that every English poet had to write a nightingale poem. You can draw your own conclusions about the conclusions the poets draw, but the inescapable fact is that birdsong moves people very much and the great bravura performers like the skylark and the nightingale provoke great people to reach for great words.

John Keats's "Ode to A Nightingale" is the most famous, with one of the great intros of all time:

My heart aches and a drowsy numbness pains
My sense, as though of hemlock I had drunk…

This is an interesting gloss on the scientific suggestion that the song of the male nightingale has a chemical effect on the brain of the female. Keats heard the bird in Hampstead and wrote the poem, so the story goes, in a single day. Pity there are no longer nightingales in Hampstead to inspire the intelligentsia who live there. Keats took his powerful response to the most powerful singer on our shores and turned it into a meditation on the unsatisfactory nature of pleasure and the inevitability

of mortality, being "half in love with easeful death".
He sees himself dead and buried, with the nightingale
singing over him:

Thou wast not born for death, immortal Bird!

Samuel Taylor Coleridge quotes and repudiates John
Milton's view on nightingales:

And hark! The nightingale begins its song.
"Most musical, most melancholy" Bird!
A melancholy bird? O idle thought!
In nature there is nothing melancholy.

One of the odd things about bird poetry is that so
often, the poet's response to the bird and its song are
considered, at least by the poet, far more interesting and
important than the bird itself. It's not the bird but the
bird's *meaning* that matters. The bird has to be a symbol,
an emblem. The entire point of the bird's existence
seems to be to cast light upon some human problem:
as if the bird itself had no relevance (like a tree falling
in a deserted forest) unless it said something about the
human condition.

John Milton turned his thoughts to love:

Thy liquid notes that close the eye of day
First heard before the shallow cuckoo's bill
Portend success in love…

John Clare was always more interested than most other poets in the birds as birds rather than symbols, and as usual, produced what is not the best poem but the best celebration of the actual bird:

> ...all the live-long day
> As though she lived on song...
> Mouth wide open to release her heart
> Of its out-sobbing songs.

Love and the nightingale are inextricable in the human mind: but that makes good ornithological sense. The song – certainly to human ears – seems to be about love, both in the sense of intense emotion and in the urgent need for intense physical expression of those emotions. That is surely at the heart of the song of the real, rather than the imagined, nightingale. It would not do to take such a thought any further, but the song – regardless of what human meaning you put onto it – requires the most colossal physical commitment. The production of such a song demands a bird's total effort for the few short weeks of its duration, with little pause even for feeding. Bluffers are weeded out almost from the start. The bird puts its life on the line to sing as it does, and that intense physical commitment communicates itself – without need for anthropomorphism – to listening humans.

Romeo and Juliet's night of passion was brought to an end by the dawn chorus. Juliet says:

Wilt thou be gone? It is not yet day.
It was the nightingale and not the lark
That pierced the fearful hollow of thine ear.
Nightly she sings in yon pomegranate tree,
Believe me, love, it was the nightingale.

Romeo replies:

It was the lark and herald of the morn,
No nightingale...
Farewell, farewell, one kiss and I'll descend... "

The singing nightingale was, as you will have noticed, considered to be female. She was thought to be suffering the unbearable pains of love, and so she drove a thorn into her heart as she sang:

She, poor bird, as all forlorn
Leans her breast up-till a thorn.

This from a poem by the 17th-century poet Richard Barnfield.

But I'll leave this celebration of love – love for both humans and nightingales – with a simple, charming and erotic poem by everybody's favourite poet, Anon. John Dowland set it to the music of the lute.

The dark is my delight;
So 'tis the nightingale's.

My music's in the night;
So is the nightingale's.
My body is but little;
So is the nightingale's.
I like to sleep next prickle;
So doth the nightingale.

Sweet music

We are not alone. That is the inescapable conclusion we reach after immersing ourselves in birdsong. The songs and calls of birds are with us almost everywhere we go, even in cities, and throughout the year. The sound of the birds encapsulates the landscape: it is the sound the landscape makes; it is the protein of the landscape that drives it.

Birds are not only wonderfully visible, but wonderfully audible as well. They are the animals we are most aware of, apart from ourselves. They are the best studied and the best loved. The sound of birds tells us that we share our planet: that we do not and cannot operate on our own.

I hope that, by reading this book and listening to the podcast, your awareness of the number of different birds that live all around us will have undergone a revolution: that you will hear great spotted woodpeckers as you take a short cut across the park, that you will hear song thrush and robin on the train station, that in the garden you will not only hear robin and blackbird, you will also hear dunnock and blackcap.

As you listen to birds, and as you look at birds, as you

become more aware of birds, so you will find yourself more aware of the differences between species. Even this book, which concentrates on a few and the most obvious species, is a celebration of biodiversity. A standard field guide will throw at you more species of birds than you will ever see or ever be able to separate, unless you turn yourself into a top operator in this field.

But the unknown hundreds and the unknowable thousands from the 10,000 species of birds across the world are all the more thrilling for being unreachable. The fact that life comes in so many forms is the most exciting thing on earth, and one that is most easily understood by listening to birds: to walk though a wood and notice a dozen species where before you may have only been aware of one or two.

And another thing: we are not alone in what we consider the uniqueness and the isolation of the human condition. As we listen to birds, we constantly come across those grey bits, those transition areas, that buffer zone, that ecotone that lies between one accepted truth and another. Humans are humans and birds are birds: but how hard and how fast are the barriers that we have, throughout history, insisted on building between ourselves and every other living thing on earth?

Music is something we all respond to, whether it's Bach or The Beatles, whether the composer is Mozart or a starling. Music is part of almost everybody's life: we are moved beyond words by the greatest pieces of music and stirred into foot-tapping merriment by a great song. When we are happy, we set about the day's chores with a song on our lips. And birds sing too. Blackbirds and humans: we are both musical creatures; we both respond to music; we both make music.

This connection between humans and other forms of life is not a matter of sentimentality. It is biology. We are connected to birds by common ancestors of the deep past and by the planet we share right now: that is to say, both by evolution and by ecology. But we are also bound together by circumstance and by our taste for rhythm and melody.

We are all creative beings. We create in the work we do, in the chores we take on: to cook a great meal and to construct a great shelf are both creative acts. Birds create nests and they create song. Argue if you like whether or not birds are conscious artists, but certainly they are creative beings, and the creative part of ourselves responds in fellowfeeling to the more creative of the repertoire singers. To deny a bird its creativity seems to me as futile, as much of a non-argument, as to deny the beauty of its song.

We can reach out our empathy beyond our own species and into the life of birds, into their world of colour and sound, because it's the same sensory world that we inhabit. As a result, we can achieve a far better intuitive understanding of the way that life on this planet operates. By listening to birds, we become aware that life doesn't work by making one super-species and letting all the rest go hang, but by means of a complex web of many, many different kinds of things. We are part of a continuum: of creativity, of understanding, of life. And as we listen to birdsong, we can reach that understanding with our hearts, our minds, our guts and our souls, and what's more, we can rejoice in it.

Listen out. Listen out for meaning, listen out for truth, listen out for life. Listen out for the birds.

Index of Birds

In case of difficulty in purchasing any Short Books
title through normal channels, please contact
BOOKPOST Tel: 01624 836000
Fax: 01624 837033
email: bookshop@enterprise.net
www.bookpost.co.uk
Please quote ref. 'Short Books'